CHARLO

Triumphant Workington Town captain Paul Charlton shows off the Lancashire Cup after leading his side to a 16-13 victory over Wigan in 1977.

CHARLO

The Story of a Rugby League Great

by

Amanda Little

© Amanda Little

ISBN 0 9534574 0 0

The right of Amanda Little to be identified as the author of this work
has been asserted by her in accordance with the
Copyright, Designs & Patents Act 1988.

All rights reserved.
No part of this book may be reproduced in any form
without the permission in writing of the author,
Amanda Little.

Printed by: Dixon Printing Co. Ltd., Kendal, Cumbria

To Joyce and Bill Little

For when the One Great Scorer comes
To write against your name,
He marks – not that you won or lost –
But how you played the game.

Grantland Rice

Amanda Little is a sports journalist with Cumbrian Newspapers in Carlisle where she has worked since 1989. She has won awards for journalistic excellence, including the prestigious NUJ North-West sports writer of the year and BNFL/Guild of Editors North-West sports writer of the year. Amanda spent two years as a football correspondent covering the affairs of Carlisle United and is now a general sports writer/sub-editor. She reports on a wide range of sports including golf, athletics, football and horse racing.
A miner's daughter from Ashington, Northumberland, she now lives in Carlisle.
This is her first book to be published.

CONTENTS

	Pages
Introduction	ix
Foreword	xi
A Star is born	1
The Early Years	5
An Age Of Innocence	9
The Impossible Dream	13
Kells Nursery School	17
The First Step	21
Debut Boy	27
One For The Future	31
The Big Time Beckons	51
A Growing Reputation	55
The World In His Hands	59
Try, Try, Try Again	65
A Man For All Seasons	69
Lions Go Into The Den	73
The Lions Roar At Last	79
Home Sweet Home	85
A Team Of Cumbrian Heroes	103
Town's Cup Of Joy	107
The Mentor	111
The Sands Of Time	115
A Task Too Tough	119
From Cumbria Coast To Gold Coast	123
A Chip Off The Old Block	127
Family Fortunes	131
Back In The Hot Seat	135
So Near Yet So Far	155
Pastures New	159
Back to the Future	161
Today's Game	163
The Charlton All-Stars	167
Tributes	173
Statistics	181
Acknowledgements	187

INTRODUCTION

THE battered old blue Ford Fiesta chugged into the pub car park, then spluttered to a halt.

The rusty door creaked open and out stepped Paul Charlton.

We were meeting to talk about the book I would write on his career.

Paul, as so many people had told me, was one of Rugby League's all-time greats, who had won virtually every honour in the game.

But that car! It was the most unlikely conveyance for someone once sold for a world record fee for a full-back, and who won 19 Great Britain caps.

Surely a man who had enjoyed the same kind of adulation in Rugby League as Bobby Charlton or Denis Law had in football, should be arriving in a flash, top-of-the-range BMW or Mercedes?

But, as I later discovered, Paul made his name in a sport where men put their bodies on the line for far less-worldly pleasures than money. It was for the love of Rugby League and a chance to satisfy their will to win.

He belonged to an era when big-money contracts and lucrative sponsorship deals were unheard of.

What I also learned was that Paul was a superstar minus any superstar pretensions. The trappings of wealth and material benefits he could have made from Rugby League were unlikely to interest him.

He grew up in a poor family on a close-knit West Cumbrian council estate. All he wanted to do from an early age was play professional Rugby League like his boyhood hero Dick Huddart.

Money was a secondary consideration.

Paul's motivation in life was simply to be a successful Rugby League player, but even he could not have foreseen how great he would become.

He was captain of both Workington Town and Cumberland. His style of captaincy echoed his style of play – inspirational, courageous and disciplined.

Only six men in the history of the sport have played more first-class games than Paul's 727 in a career which lasted nearly 20 years.

He holds the record for appearances in a Workington Town shirt. By the time he played his last game for the club at Widnes on December 28, 1980, he had totted up 419 appearances.

He also represented Cumberland more times than any other player. Not even Workington idols Ike Southward, Brian Edgar and Billy Ivison could match his 32 appearances for the county.

In 1969 Paul became the world's costliest full-back when he was transferred from Workington to Salford for £12,500.

But, while many sportsmen buckled under the weight of hefty transfer fees, Paul's game positively flourished in the spotlight.

He was widely-acknowledged as the greatest full-back of his generation. The game has never seen a full-back who scored tries in such a torrent. No full-back has come near matching his record of 223 career tries. Nor have they come close to breaking his record tally of 33 tries in a season.

Then there were his international appearances. He made more appearances for Great Britain than any other Workington Town player, even the legendary Gus Risman.

The well-thumbed scrapbooks, proudly compiled by Paul's father Harold, contain faded newspaper cuttings, giving a further fascinating insight into his career.

They provided me with more background for the book. There were reports of big matches featuring some of the world's greatest players – Langlands, Beetson, Fulton, Watkins and Hesketh.

But then there were still many unanswered questions. They could only be answered by Paul himself, his family, friends and former team-mates.

I needed to know what made him the prolific try-scorer, the inspirational captain.

What emerged was his discipline, commitment and total dedication to Rugby League.

Yet despite the success and adulation, Paul remains unspoiled. His modesty prevents him from fully realising the high esteem he is held in by those around him.

After the earlier meeting with him, one important point of contact was Rugby League historian Robert Gate, a walking encyclopaedia on the game.

Within a week, a parcel arrived full of facts and figures on Paul's career.

The statistics may not have told the full story, but they confirmed my initial belief. It was there in black and white. Clapped-out car or not, Paul Charlton is one of Rugby League's all-time greats.

FOREWORD

by Mike Stephenson

SOME people say that men never grow up. Others claim that we, the macho of the sexes, ignore the years that stick to us like the mud on your boots from all the wet grounds in Cumbria.

Let's face it, we all would like to say we never grow old and that Father Time missed us by a country mile. It's a forlorn hope, of course. It never works out that way but, if there's one bloke who has put all such theories to the test, it has to be my old 'Marra' Paul Charlton.

I honestly know one Mr P. Charlton will never grow up. And quite frankly, I wouldn't expect him to either. He's one big, likeable kid!

It wasn't that long ago he was pushing his fitness and body to the limits by playing top grade Rugby League at an age when most people would be content to sit back in the old rocking chair, telling exaggerated tales about deeds on the playing fields of Rugby League.

Unless I'm mistaken, he's probably still trying to bamboozle some defence with his body swerve and dummy, even if it's just touch and pass! I reckon he'll be out there somewhere hail, rain or shine.

One of the all-time favourite sons of Cumbria, he will always be classed, not just as a great Rugby League player, but a great bloke who gave his fellow players, fans, club officials and even the opposition so much pleasure in his many years of playing the greatest game of all.

I once overheard one of my old Dewsbury team-mates comment that if there was one bloke he didn't mind not being able to stop from scoring, it was that bloke with the funny face and the weird accent!

He had determination, the will to win attitude and a heart so big it would probably match his huge fee he got when he signed for the high-flying Salford side nearly 30 years ago.

There was little doubt you could also rely on that same full-back hero when it came down to being the last line of defence for his club, county or country. Seeing this talented player walking back with a huge grin on his face after scoring tries was a delight.

Obviously, it was more of a thrill if you were on the same side, and I had the privilege to play alongside Paul in that World Cup winning side of 1972, when we beat the Aussies in Lyon against all the odds to run the lap of honour with the 'Coup du Monde'.

Incidentally, it was a cup so big that 'Marra' used it to help smuggle a few bottles of extra duty-free brandy back into England!

I can also remember missing a tackle on the great Aussie icon

Bobby Fulton in extra-time of the final.

It was one of the few occasions we allowed 'Bozo,' who was at the time classed as the best player in the world, to break free. My heart sank but without much fuss 'Charlo' ensured he pushed Fulton out towards the corner and took him down with a superb match-saving tackle into touch.

He not only saved my bacon but the team's as well. I can remember him saying something to me as I slowly made my way towards the scrum and, you know, I couldn't understand a bloody word he said. I think it was something like: "Don't worry, he was no problem!"

That just about sums up the man. No problem. He just moulded into everything as though he'd been part of the team for years.

Rugby League players are often put into one class or another. Tough, fast, creative, etc., etc. But just throw in all the plaudits you want and they would fit Paul to a tee.

In the 30 years I've known him, I can't remember him losing his temper, although I once saw him a little angry.

It occurred while he was staying with me in Australia during one of his many trips Down Under. I was away at work at the ABC office when he rang me to say a telegram had arrived for me and it was marked private and urgent.

"Open it," I said.

"I can't do that, it's not for me", he replied.

After much persuasion, he ripped the telegram open, which read as follows.

"Mr Stephenson. Your contract from today has been terminated with the Australian Broadcasting TV Commission. Do not turn up for the televised match this Saturday."

"What does that mean", enquired Paul.

"It appears they have just given me an offer I can't refuse", I replied.

"Like what?"

"Like the sack".

Paul went off like a rocket because they didn't have the guts to tell me to my face. He was far from impressed. It was nice to know he felt for me so much. A truly great mate.

I'm sure by the time you've read this book you'll feel he is a mate of yours too.

And if you're sitting comfortably on the sofa, make sure there's a space clear next to you. Knowing 'Marra,' he's more than likely to plonk himself down beside you. He's just that type of bloke.

A STAR IS BORN

JOSEPHINE Charlton could feel herself trembling as tears began to well up in her eyes. Unable to think straight, she ran outside and looked frantically up and down the street.

Coach Road in Whitehaven with its row of miners' houses was deserted apart from an old man slowly cycling along the lane. There was no sign of her five-year-old son Paul, who only a short time earlier had been playing happily with the other children in the street.

Her brother John clasped her hands, which were still wet and soapy from an afternoon spent in the wash tub.

"Divven't worry lass, we'll find him," he said softly.

Josephine was a petite woman, with shoulder length dark hair and kind brown-hazel eyes. She was a gentle person, the kind everyone warmed to. She would never have a bad word said about anybody and people respected her for it. A strong Catholic, she never missed church on a Sunday, apart from when her chronic bronchitis flared up in the winter. Josephine was the backbone of her family and she adored her children.

Paul had been born at home on December 6, 1941. Fifteen months later, their daughter Jean was born. Josephine and her husband Harold planned to have more children soon, even if it meant further financial sacrifice.

Harold, a miner at William Colliery, had scrimped and saved to buy Paul a second-hand bike. It was falling to pieces and rusty when he'd bought it, but Harold had spent a week hidden away in his garden shed lovingly restoring it. Paul had been riding the bike in Coach Road before he vanished.

He was a bright, lively child with a naturally inquisitive mind. He was also a wanderer, who often took off without warning but it never stopped Josephine from worrying about what might have happened to him.

He had inherited wanderlust from his grandfather Robert Charlton who lived on High Road in Kells. Each Saturday Josephine would fix Paul a packed lunch of home-made bread, cheese and an apple, and he and his grandfather would catch the bus to Ennerdale, before setting out on a walk around the picturesque valley in the heart of West Cumbria. Paul enjoyed the outdoor life and also loved to join Harold's brother-in-law Jim Fowler on fishing trips to Whitehaven Pier.

As Josephine cast another anxious look down Coach Road to

Jackson's Timber Yard, she spotted one of Paul's friends running towards her. She didn't know his name but his face was familiar as one of the kids in the street who played with Paul.

"Mrs Charlton," he gasped. "It's Paul. I think he's fallen in't watter."

Josephine's mind was racing, then suddenly she remembered the pond just off Coach Road. She hurried off down the street with John close behind her towards the pond just beside the railway line. But just before she got to the railway crossing, she suddenly caught a glimpse of a small child sitting happily in the signal box. She instantly recognised the tousled blond hair and impish grin of her oldest child as he sat alongside Dick, the one-legged signalman, his eyes dancing with excitement as he fiddled with the controls.

Dick's signal box was a magnet for the local children, particularly Paul. He was fascinated by railways and dreamed of becoming a train driver. Every day he would cross the railway line on his way to St Mary's Junior School in Kells. Dick, a small man in his 50s, would hobble along on his artificial leg to open the gates, touch the peak of his flat cap and wave to the children on their way to school. The signal box was only about 300 yards from Paul's house, and not far from the Recreation Ground, the home of Whitehaven Rugby League Club, which was soon to become another focus of the young Charlton's attentions.

★ ★ ★

Josephine and Harold were spending their evening together talking quietly. It was shortly before nine o'clock and they had only just put the children to bed. It was their chance to unwind and enjoy the peace and quiet which was a rare luxury in a household full of the noise which went with two boisterous children.

Suddenly they heard footsteps coming down the creaky staircase and along the hallway. Paul popped his head around the living room door.

"Dad, there's something hairy in my bed."

Harold looked at Josephine and winked, before taking Paul by the hand and leading him back upstairs to the bedroom. Harold checked Paul's bed, looking underneath the woollen blankets but, as he expected, there was nothing there.

"There's nowt there lad, you've just had a bad dream," reassured Harold, kissing his son tenderly on the head, before tucking him back up in bed.

Harold studied the hole in the wall just beneath the window, which he hadn't got round to fixing and promised himself he'd do it before winter set in. The following day Josephine was cleaning the house upstairs when suddenly she caught sight of a huge black rat with a long tail scurrying into Paul's bedroom.

Paul had been right. There was something hairy in his bedroom. Jackson's timber yard in Coach Road was alive with rats and it was clear that one of them had managed to find its way into the house.

The next day Harold arrived home from work with a terrier he had borrowed from one of his workmates. While Josephine and the kids stayed downstairs, a safe distance from the rat, which still sent shivers down their spines, Harold disappeared upstairs with the dog, which he had been assured would have no bother dispensing with it.

Harold, who was also armed with a shovel, spotted the rat's tail sticking out from behind the old wooden wardrobe in the corner of the room. Very gently, he eased the wardrobe to one side. Quick as a flash, the rat darted out towards the terrier, which sat rooted to the spot. The rat then sprang at the dog, biting it on the mouth and, as Harold lunged at the rat with his shovel, it scurried out of the way and the heavy shovel came crashing down on the hapless terrier's head. As the dog yelped and ran out the room with its tail between its legs, Harold managed to strike the rat and end its brief reign of terror.

THE EARLY YEARS

WHITEHAVEN was one of the poorest communities in the country. In the mid-19th century, a damning report by Sir Robert Rawlinson, superintending inspector to the General Health Board, summed up the conditions in the West Cumbria town.

"I have no hesitation in asserting that there is no English town with which I am acquainted where the sanitary circumstances of the inhabitants, and especially the poor, are in a more disgraceful and degrading condition", he wrote.

"Amid these scenes of utter destitution, misery and extreme degradation in Whitehaven there are, however, instances of a desire for cleanliness, even in some of the worst places and it is most painful to contemplate the hopeless position of such persons, who are generally English and have known better times and happier days."

The filth and squalor of property at the turn of the century had forced the town council to set up a housing committee to see what could be done about providing better working class houses. It led to 80 houses being built on Coach Road, where the Charltons lived after moving from Woodhouse shortly after Paul's birth in 1941. They later returned to live on the Woodhouse estate and settled in Fell View Avenue.

The prosperity of the town hinged on the bustling harbour and the mines, the biggest of which was William Colliery, near Bransty. The Whitehaven coalfield was divided into two main sections. One embraced the vast tract lying between the St Bees valley and the Irish Sea. The other lay to the north-east of the same valley.

Disasters were common. Hundreds of brave men, forced down the pit at an early age through tradition and necessity, had lost their lives, including 104 in the William Pit disaster of 1947. But for the grace of God, Harold might well have been working down the mine that day. He had only just returned to work as a miner at William Colliery. A few years earlier he had been badly hurt in an underground accident. Two huge tubs of coal broke loose and careered down the track out of control, smashing into Harold's back and chipping his spine.

After recuperating, the pain was still too much for him to return to the pit and he got a job as a chauffeur for a local doctor. He then worked for Phillip's Warehouse, delivering food. It was much lighter work than the hard graft down the pit but the pay wasn't as good. Shortly after the war, his back was much stronger and he went to work at William Pit. The future of the pit was bleak and there had been talk of closure. It was a constant worry for Harold and Josephine.

Harold was a devoted family man. Strong as an ox from the years in the mine, he was also strong on discipline and determined his children would grow up with good manners and respect for others. But he also possessed a gentle nature and would often go without to make sure Josephine and the children could have the occasional luxury. They had added to their family when another son, Philip, was born in 1948.

Money was scarce, but Harold topped up his pay by playing the accordion in a local four-piece band called the Delphenians. The quartet toured the working men's clubs and dance halls all over Cumbria four nights a week, playing music of the era, tangos, the rumba and foxtrots. He made ten bob (50p) a week and he and his family had come to rely on the extra money.

It was from his income as a part-time musician that he was able to put away a few bob each week to buy his children the occasional treat. Birthdays usually just came and went because they simply did not have the money to buy presents. Christmas, on the other hand, was always such a happy day in the Charlton household, though they could never afford anything extravagant.

★ ★ ★

It was Christmas Eve and the house was full of excited chatter and laughter. The tinsel glistened in the firelight as Harold, Paul and his brother and sister sat warming themselves by the hearth. Josephine was busy in the kitchen making sure she had everything for the dinner she had planned for the next day.

First she and the children would take the short walk to St Begh's Church, where they worshipped. After that it was time to open their parcels which had been left at the bottom of their bed, then they would all tuck into a traditional Christmas dinner. Turkey, stuffing and all the trimmings, followed by Josephine's home-made Christmas pudding.

Harold and Josephine waited until the children were sleeping, before they quietly carried the presents out of their wardrobe and left them at the bottom of their beds, ready for when they awoke the next morning. They used to love to watch the expressions on their young faces as they ripped open their presents. Paul was woken from his sleep by the noise coming from his younger brother and sister. He was 13 and no longer believed in Father Christmas but that didn't stop him getting excited.

Harold had found his oldest railway-crazy child the ideal present.

He had scrimped and saved for weeks to buy him a spanking new toy train but he had been unable to afford the rails to go with it. Then he had hit on an ingenious idea. He had seen a set of rails in a local junk shop, and bought them to go with the train. Josephine found a cardboard box, put the train and rails inside and wrapped it ready for Christmas morning.

As Paul roused from his slumber, he spotted the parcel at the bottom of his bed and carefully picked it up. He peeled off the paper, before carefully opening the box. His eyes lit up at what he saw. Lifting one of the sections of tracks out of the box, he carefully placed the train on top of it, only to discover the train didn't fit. Harold's heart sank. Weeks of careful planning had ended in disappointment.

But Paul was not the sort of boy to get upset over a toy train and a few lengths of railway track. His dad had tried his best to make him happy. Surely that alone was enough to earn him admiration and respect.

AN AGE OF INNOCENCE

THE scrap of waste land behind Woodhouse estate was a barren wilderness to most of the residents living on the estate, but to the dozen-or-so kids who flocked there after school, it was a field of dreams. The grass, once lush-green and ankle high, had long since been worn away by small feet wearing tatty brown boots which pounded up and down for hours on end.

The makeshift pitch was marked only by a pile of coats and jumpers which slowly diminished as, one by one, the youngsters were called home for bed. Once the teams had been picked by two self-appointed captains, the rough and tumble would begin.

Most of the children attended Whitehaven Secondary Modern, while others, like Paul, went to St Begh's Roman Catholic School. At St Begh's they were taught the basics of Rugby League in PE lessons on Wednesday afternoons, under the careful guidance of teacher Ged Worsley. They would play against other schools in the area like Distington, Richmond and Kells, but it was on their home territory that their love of the game was able to flourish. The rules were basic but many was the time a game of touch rugby would erupt into a no-holds-barred free-for-all with a few eye-watering tackles. Fun and laughter were as important as winning and a lifetime's memories were built on that patch of scrub land.

All the children lived on Fell View Avenue. There was Alf Williams, Harold 'Tag' Roberts, brothers Tom and Joe Walker, Les Cowell, Raymond 'Gosh' Reeves, Robert 'Boots' Henderson and his brother Albert 'Tabby' Henderson. For many of the youngsters their ambition by far outweighed their talent, but for one, that piece of waste land was to provide the platform for his dream of a professional Rugby League career.

Thirteen-year-old Paul Charlton was small for his age, some might even have said scrawny, but there was something special about him which made him stand out from the rest. A few years earlier, he wouldn't have been given a second glance, but by the time he had reached his teens, a natural talent, however raw, was emerging. Scouts from Whitehaven Rugby League Club would regularly stand on the touchline watching the youngsters eagerly trying to impress on their humble stage.

Paul was starting to become a regular spectator at Whitehaven's Recreation Ground, where he had first been taken by his grandad as a nipper. Crowds of around 6,000 would pack into the ground and it was awe-inspiring for a young child. Watching what was going on around him on the terrace was often more enthralling to Paul than the action on the pitch but as long as he had his pop, a bag of sweets or the occasional pie, he was quiet and content while his grandad concentrated on the game. Gradually though, the activity on the field began to hold more appeal as Paul grew a little older, until he became fascinated by it.

Dick Huddart, Billy McAlone and John McKeown were among Whitehaven's stars of the fifties and Paul and his friends would practise re-creating their skills when they got home from matches to the field behind their homes. Huddart was a particular favourite of Paul's. The second row forward was a Flimby lad with a tremendous turn of pace who later became a member of the all-conquering Great Britain tour of Australia in 1958. Paul would often imagine he was Huddart on the back playing field, while his friends would pretend to be other Whitehaven players.

The cuts and bumps and bruises quickly became part and parcel of the play. The main danger was the regular clip around the ear Paul would get from Harold when he got home with his jumper torn and his best pair of pants caked in mud. He'd be put straight into the tin bath to scrub the muck off his knees, elbows and face, while Josephine would set about washing his clothes in the dolly tub, before putting them through the mangle. Then she could start the task of stitching them back together again.

When the game was over, the children would often head back to Paul's house at number 76 or to Alf's, across the road at number 89. Josephine or Alf's mother, Margaret, would give them all a slice of jam and bread washed down by a glass of home-made lemonade. When the boys weren't playing on the back field, they would find other pursuits to occupy their time. In the summer they would often head for Whitehaven beach to play on the sand dunes and rock pools at Barrowmouth or further along at Saltom Beach. The old cemetery, near the quarry, was also a big attraction for the boys. Perched precariously on each other's backs, they would knock the conkers from the trees until they were chased out of the graveyard by the local bobby, Sergeant Lister.

There was a strong sense of community spirit in Fell View Avenue. The Queen's Coronation was marked by the locals with a huge street party. All the women clubbed together to bake cakes and biscuits. Then they presented sandwiches and huge jugs of orange and lemonade for the children, who wore red, white and blue and waved flags.

There were also bus trips arranged, where the parents would club together for the youngsters to have a day away at the seaside or at Blackpool illuminations. In many ways it was an idyllic childhood in an age of innocence.

★ ★ ★

The county schools selectors had made their final decision as to which youngsters would be in the team to play Yorkshire at Leeds. They had been watching school games for the last couple of weeks and had also heard the recommendations of the games masters.

Paul had talked about nothing else for days, and Harold and Josephine knew how much it meant to him to be chosen to play for the county. Josephine was pacing the living room floor waiting for her oldest child to return from school with news of the team when suddenly she heard the front door swing open. Paul walked into the room, and she didn't need to ask. The answer was written all over his face. His name was not on the team sheet.

Harold put a comforting arm around his son's shoulders but nothing could help soften the blow. Later that evening while his friends from the neighbourhood headed for the Gaiety Cinema to watch the latest cowboy film, Paul could be found alone on the playing field behind his home, kicking the ball into the air and catching it on the run, before sprinting towards an imaginary try-line. There and then he vowed he'd never be second best again.

★ ★ ★

The early autumn sun was setting behind the pit head-gear and the game was finally over for another night. The tired youngsters collected their coats and began to troop off the pitch. Paul was just tying his jacket round his waist ready for the short walk home to Fell View Avenue when he was called over by two men standing at the edge of the field. He recognised their faces as he'd seen them once before standing on the touchline.

One was Henry Brown, who lived across the road and played full-back for local amateur side, Kells. They were the best side in the Cumberland Rugby League and had spawned many professional players. Henry was in his early-20s, a small player but well built. He was a regular in the Kells side and was tipped to play for the Great Britain amateur side.

"You had a good game, son," said Henry. "Look after yourself and keep working hard and you could have a future in the game."

Paul could feel the hairs on the back of his neck standing up and he beamed with pride. "Thanks mister," he said grinning broadly from ear to ear, before running to catch up with his young pals.

THE IMPOSSIBLE DREAM

MOST working class youngsters followed their fathers down the mines of West Cumbria, but Josephine was determined she wanted a better life for her oldest son. Although a bright lad with a sharp inquiring mind, Paul was no academic and Josephine and Harold could not have afforded for him to carry on his education even if he had wanted to. He was a quiet boy, with a hint of natural shyness, respectful and well-behaved. It was the way Josephine and Harold had brought him up.

On leaving Class 4A at St Begh's, his form teacher Cyril Rooney wrote in his final report: "Paul is a hard-working, conscientious pupil who has been a pleasure to teach and I'm sure he will go on and do well in life."

Josephine saw a job advertised in the local newspaper, *The Whitehaven News*, for a television engineer at H. L. Elliott in Lowther Street, and persuaded Paul to go for the interview. The family didn't even own a television. It was a luxury only the well-off could afford. They only knew one family on the Woodhouse estate who owned one. They lived in Buttermere Avenue, and would charge people to go and sit in their living room to watch it. Paul reluctantly agreed to attend the interview at H. L. Elliott, even though his mind was firmly focused elsewhere.

Whitehaven Rugby League Club had set up a B team two years earlier and were always on the look out for fresh, rising talent to fill the side. Paul made a deal with Josephine. He would attend the Saturday morning interview as long as he could go for a trial at the rugby ground that afternoon. The interview did not go well. They needed someone with a knowledge of electronics and, with a polite handshake, Paul was shown the front door.

That afternoon he made his way to the Recreation Ground. It was a familiar walk. By now he was a die-hard fan who never missed a game, even though his grandfather had passed away.

Paul, Alf Williams and Les Steele sold programmes on match days. They would pick them up on Saturday lunchtime from Todd's Printers on Strand Street, before catching the bus to Coach Road. Paul would stand at the main gate, Alf would stand at the park gates end of Coach Road, while Les had the prime position at the other end of Coach Road, where most supporters would buy their programmes. The programmes cost 3p and for every 100 sold the boys earned commission. It was only a few shillings pocket money, but it was enough to be able to buy a cup of Bovril and a meat pie or a packet of crisps at half time from the old bus which was used as a stall. Once their afternoon's work was done they would be ready to catch the second half.

Whitehaven were coached at the time by Billy Little. Little was a former miner from Great Clifton, who had played Rugby Union for Workington Zebras, before switching codes to play amateur Rugby League with Great Clifton. A scrum-half, he signed professionally for Barrow in 1932 and went on to become an automatic choice for Cumberland for the next decade. His reputation as a Craven Park legend was guaranteed in 1938 when he kicked a last-minute, long-range drop goal which put Barrow in their first Wembley final at the expense of Halifax. When his Barrow career ended, he accepted the coaching post at the Recreation Ground.

The Whitehaven B team played in Division One of the Cumberland Rugby League. It was pre-season and the second team were short of players for the new campaign. Even though he was only 15, Paul spotted his chance of staking a claim for a place in the side. The training sessions were tough, but Paul enjoyed every minute and learned a lot. The first team trained with them and it was a huge thrill for Paul to stand alongside players he looked up to and respected. But his time with Whitehaven proved shortlived. With the new season just weeks away, it was announced the B team would fold because of a shortage of players.

★ ★ ★

Paul began work as a delivery boy for the launderette on Low Road, returning the neatly-pressed piles of washing to customers living nearby. It was a stop-gap job until something better came up. Josephine and Harold were keen for their son to learn a trade as a builder, electrician or plumber.

After just 10 weeks at the launderette, Paul started as a labourer at the Whitehaven brickworks, further down Low Road. It was as if he was destined to fall into a series of dead-end jobs. His weekly wage was £3 two shillings and sixpence (£3.13) and every Friday night, without a moment's hesitation, he would hand it over to Josephine, who gave him back some pocket money before putting the rest into the family budget.

For long nine-hour shifts, Paul wheeled barrows full of bricks from the scorching kilns, before loading them by hand on to the builders' wagons. The work was back-breaking and soul-destroying, but out of the dust, dirt and sweat, a man was beginning to emerge.

The brickworks overlooked the Recreation Ground and every now and then during a brief break from his punishing labours, Paul would gaze longingly over the road where the white goal posts were clearly visible. If he shut his eyes for a moment, he could picture himself pulling on a Whitehaven shirt and running on to the pitch in front of thousands of supporters. Yet his Rugby League career seemed as ready to get started as a battered, old car on a winter's morning. It was his lifelong ambition, but as he started loading up another lorry load of bricks, it seemed like an impossible dream.

KELLS NURSERY SCHOOL

HENRY Brown was not only a talented Rugby League player himself, he also had an eye for spotting up-and-coming young players. He knew almost as soon as he had seen Paul Charlton playing on the back field behind Woodhouse estate that here was a star in the making.

Henry lived in Fell View Avenue, opposite Alfie Williams, and after leaving Whitehaven Grammar School, began work as an apprentice at the nearby chemical plant, Marchon. Stocky and well-built, he was first choice full-back for Kells in the Cumberland Amateur Rugby League. He won amateur honours when he represented England against France at Leeds in 1954 and against Italy at Halifax.

The amateur team was a fore-runner to the British Amateur Rugby League Association and the team which played France had contained three other Cumbrians – Hensingham scrum-half Sol Roper, Egremont prop Jimmy Logan and Henry's Kells team-mate, prop Harry Crewdson. Henry played a starring role in England's first victory over France in 20 years when he kicked two goals in their 23-0 win. They followed up the success with a hard-fought 18-11 victory over Italy.

Henry would often lean on the fence at the bottom of his parents' garden and watch the game of tag rugby going on in the back field. He had heard about Whitehaven B team folding and how disappointed Paul had been so he had encouraged him to go along to a training session at Kells. Kells Under-19 team, who played in the Whitehaven and District League, were on the look out for a new full-back and he believed it was a position ideally suited to Paul, even though the teenager had spent his school years playing hooker.

Brown was planning to go and live in Canada, where his employers Albright & Wilson had several other plants. He had carried his dreams of emigrating to Canada from childhood. His aunty Ginnie lived in Vancouver, and every Christmas she sent over a food parcel, containing treats for the family, which were not available in Britain during the war years.

It would contain a Christmas cake, sugar cubes, chocolate bars for Henry and his two brothers and sisters, and the most delicious butter-scotch puddings, the likes of which the family had never tasted. During a time when many children were being evacuated, Ginnie had even suggested the five Brown children went to live with her until the war was over. But Henry's parents had insisted the family would not be broken up.

When Henry married his girlfriend Elsie, she shared his dream of moving to Canada and by sheer coincidence, the chance to transfer to the Albright & Wilson plant over there came up. Aged 39, Henry and Elsie flew from Prestwick Airport with four of their young children into the unknown to begin a new life thousands of miles away.

★ ★ ★

It was October and the new season was already well under way when Paul attended his first training session at Kells Welfare. He already knew a few of the players – brothers Spanky and Michael McFarlane, Eddie Brennen, Phil Kitchin and Dick Morgan. Kells had a proud tradition of being a hotbed of Rugby League talent. The club was in the blood of many players; their fathers and grandfathers had also pulled on the red and white hooped shirts and black shorts. The players trained twice a week on Tuesdays and Thursdays on Kells Welfare field.

Geoff Bowden was head coach at Kells, but the mainstay of the club was Jim Kitchen. Jim was secretary, bag man, chief cook and bottle washer. He was a lifelong fan of the club, and even as a child he would attend all the games, home and away. As a youngster he would travel to the away games on the team bus, sitting on a huge basket containing the players' kits in the aisle between the seats. He was the only member of his family interested in Rugby League. He came from a strong hound-trailing family and his Uncle Joe had trained a champion hound called Mountain.

Jim, an overman at Haig Pit, even ran the administration side of the club from his home. His wife Madge also helped behind the scenes as treasurer, although she had another, equally important role at the club. Every Sunday night she washed all the kits by hand in two huge tubs in the couple's backyard, before putting them through a mangle. She would then hang them out to dry on Kells back field, then press them ready for the next weekend's games. It had long been recognised that, had it not been for the dedication and enthusiasm of the pair, Kells Rugby League Club would have long since died.

The couple met shortly after the war, where Jim had served in Norway, Egypt, North Africa, India, Ceylon and Burma. Madge, who came from Workington, had been introduced to the handsome young sergeant by her brother, Charlie Phillips, who had also served in the Territorial Army. Jim was born and brought up at 7, North Row, and the couple lived at the same address all their married life, until Madge's death in 1989. He had been chairman of Kells for six years until 1958.

He then took over as secretary with Duncan Walker, father of future Rugby League star Boxer, replacing him as chairman.

Jim was steeped in knowledge of the local amateur game, and his views on players were highly respected. Workington Town had turned to him to help sign several young players and the chairman Jim Graves had asked him to keep an eye out for other promising players. Jim was behind the transfers of three Kells players to Workington's Derwent Park - Raymond Devlin, Eddie Brennan and Matty McLeod – and he was constantly looking for new, fresh talent.

★ ★ ★

The year was 1958 and the King of Rock and Roll Elvis Presley was top of the charts with *Jailhouse Rock*. Seventeen-year-old Paul Charlton loved to spend hours in his room listening to records on his old second-hand 78 rpm gramophone, which Josephine and Harold had bought for him for Christmas when he was 15. Elvis was a particular favourite of Paul's but he was also a big fan of Lonnie Donegan's skiffle music. Donegan had been in the charts with *Gamblin' Man, Cumberland Gap* and *Lost John*, and Paul had all his records. Paul and his friends from the neighbourhood had just set up their own skiffle group. Paul played the drums, Alf Williams, Joe Walker and Les Steele guitars and Raymond Reeves double bass, which was really an old upside down tea chest with a broom attached to a piece of string.

Paul would practise for hours, banging away on the drums in the front parlour with Harold, Josephine, Jean, Philip and Robert as his audience. Harold, who was keen for his son to follow in his musical footsteps, had made him a second-hand drum set, collecting each part over several months. Once a week the band would get together for a practice session. One of their neighbours, Billy Crawford, a miner at Haig Pit, had given them permission to use the garden shed. The teenagers dreamed of fame and fortune, but the nearest they came to hitting the big time was playing a gig at the RAFA Club after being offered the chance by one of the stewards, Eric Boadle, who later became landlord at The Stump.

Sport also played a major part in Paul's life. He signed to play for Cleator in the Cumbria Cricket League, and there he developed a lifelong love for the game. At weekends he would also play table tennis at Mirehouse Youth Club. But it was on the rugby pitch where he was really beginning to stand out. He quickly established himself as a regular in the Kells Under-19 side. Josephine and Harold attended every game to cheer their son on from the touchline, even during the cruellest winters with driving rain and icy winds blowing in off the sea. Josephine would bring along the half-time oranges she had bought at Whitehaven market for every player. She would then pour herself and Harold a cuppa from the flask they took to all the games to warm them through ready for the second half.

The pace of the play and the toughness of the tackles by big, powerful players who took no prisoners were different from anything Paul had ever experienced, but his first season with the Under-19 side had been a huge success.

He had been part of the side which beat Broughton Moor to lift the County Under-19 Cup. Kells had also won the Whitehaven and District Under-19 League Championship. He had stood out in a good team by scoring 12 tries, which included two hat-tricks.

His potential had also attracted the eye of the county Under-19 selectors, Tom Stewart, Joe Tyson and Billy Proud, who had been watching local games all season to pick the team to face Lancashire and Yorkshire. Paul's name was penciled in at full-back and the county side followed up their defeat at the hands of Yorkshire at Keighley with a win over Lancashire at Maryport.

THE FIRST STEP

PAUL stood open-mouthed, barely able to take in the words Jim Kitchen had just spoken. "Billy Ivison, the Workington Town coach, wants to see you and your dad this week for a meeting. He's interested in signing you, son", said Jim.

The words ran through his head again and again, before it finally started to sink in. All Paul had thought about over the last few months was his dream of making the grade with a professional club. His lifetime's ambition was to play for Whitehaven, yet here were their bitterest rivals offering to make his dream come true.

The meeting was fixed for the following week. Paul and Harold were ushered into the boardroom where they both shook hands with Billy Ivison and the Town chairman Jim Graves. Paul tried hard to hide the feeling of being totally overawed but he couldn't help but sense he was in the presence of greatness. Here was a shy boy from a West Cumbrian council estate, unsure of his own ability, being offered the chance to join a club steeped in tradition with a proud record of producing some of the greatest Rugby League players.

Billy Ivison was one of the finest players ever to don a Workington Town jersey. Off the field, he was the perfect gentleman, kind and warm-hearted, but as soon as he pulled on his rugby boots and took to the field, he was one of the hardest competitors and fiercest tacklers in the game.

He had begun his career with Moresby Rugby Union club, before signing for Workington Town when they entered the professional ranks in 1945-46. A small, stocky loose forward, he could wreak havoc with his perfectly timed passes and he was at the centre of Town's success. His bravery and toughness were displayed in the 1951 Championship final when he helped Town to a 26-11 victory over Warrington, despite suffering a broken jaw. This Prince among Forwards possessed hands like shovels with which he could deftly slip the ball one-handed to a supporting player.

He had taken over as player-coach from Jim Brough, and quickly won the respect and admiration of his players.

In the boardroom, Graves, a local shop and cinema owner, handed Paul a piece of paper. It was a contract offering him more money than he had ever seen in his life. He had left the Whitehaven Brickworks, and was serving his time as an apprentice carpenter for James Leslie and Son, a building firm in Coach Road. The pay was about average for a 19-

year-old, but here he was being offered a huge amount for something he adored doing. The contract was worth £1,500, which was made up of a £300 signing-on fee, a further £150 after he had played six first team games and £150 after 12 first team games. It stated he would be given bonuses for county appearances, winning an England cap, a Great Britain cap and if he toured with Great Britain. Town would also pay him a weekly wage of £4 and ten shillings (£4.50) when they won and £1 and 10 shillings (£1.50) if they lost.

But money meant little to Paul. The only thing he was concerned about was that he was being given the chance to play Rugby League with a professional club. Without a moment's hesitation, he picked up the pen Graves had given him and signed at the bottom of the contract.

Paul's transfer to Town was of course reported in the local newspaper, the *Times & Star*.

"The Town have signed on professional forms the Kells and Cumberland junior full-back Paul Charlton", ran the report. "Well built and a good handler, he has proved in junior games that he has got what it takes to make a player and the Town club were only one of many who were interested in acquiring his services."

★ ★ ★

The piercing ringing of his alarm clock at 7.30 that morning jolted Paul back to earth. He remembered he still had a living to make outside Rugby League. It was Monday morning and Paul arrived at the crack of dawn to start his day's work. He still had a spring in his step from the excitement of the last few days.

James Leslie and Son had been contracted to renovate some houses on Tower Hill housing estate in Whitehaven, and Paul knew it would be the start of a busy week. First, however, he had been summoned to see the boss, Dalton Leslie, in his office. The meeting was brief and he asked to see Paul again in the afternoon, along with Harold.

After all the excitement of signing for Workington, Paul was unprepared for the ultimatum he was about to be given by his employer: Rugby League or his job as a carpenter. Mr Leslie explained to Paul and his father how they had previously employed the Whitehaven player John Temby as a bricklayer. According to Mr Leslie, Temby had been forced to miss days at work because of playing commitments and injuries. The company simply couldn't afford to risk employing another Rugby League player.

"You're going to have to make a choice", said Mr Leslie. "You can keep your job here and continue your apprenticeship, or you can play professional Rugby League". Harold looked at Paul. "It's your choice, son. What do you want to do?" he asked.

"All I've ever wanted to be is a Rugby League player and I can't give up this opportunity", replied Paul.

"Right then", said Harold. "You'll find another job but you may never get the chance to be a professional Rugby League player again, so the decision is made for you." The pair left Mr Leslie's office and headed for home.

Within a week Paul had found another firm, Border Engineers, which was also in Coach Road, to take him. The owner John Walker, a keen Rugby League fan, took over Paul's apprenticeship and he began work the following Monday. Everything had begun to fall neatly into place. Nothing could stop him now.

★ ★ ★

As soon as he stepped onto the training pitch, Paul could sense that the only way was up. He was surrounded by great players, and he knew he could only learn from them. Paul's arrival at Town coincided with the return to Derwent Park of the great Ike Southward, who rejoined the club for a second spell from Oldham. He had swapped the rural beauty of Cumbria for the industrial grime of Lancashire when Oldham signed him for a world record fee of £10,650 in 1959. His 11 Test caps between 1958 and 1962 were testimony to his reputation as one of the greatest wingers in the world. Southward had been a member of the Town side which finished runners-up in the 1955 and 1958 Challenge Cup final. They had lost 21-12 to Barrow in 1955 at Wembley and again were forced to settle for runners-up place three years later when they were beaten 13-9 by Wigan.

Town were captained by Sol Roper, a veteran of both cup finals. Roper, who hailed from Pica, was regarded by many as the best uncapped scrum-half. Cocky and confident, he was a strong decision-maker, who led the side by example. Then there was prop forward Brian Edgar, a gentle giant off the field, but a hard man on it with a powerful turn of speed. The former Cockermouth Grammar School pupil had first represented England Schools at Rugby Union and had gone on to become a star with Great Britain at Rugby League.

There were also two new signings from South Africa in the side, Piet Pretorius and Jacob Ferreira. The season before Paul signed they had won 22 consecutive games, and were a real force in the game.

The players trained twice a week under Ivison, a hard task-master, who had them warming up by running around the field, before sprint training, running with weights and a game of touch rugby.

Paul stepped straight into the 'A' team, which was run by former player Billy Miller. His debut was at home to Widnes in front of a sparse crowd, which included Josephine and Harold and Jim and Madge Kitchen. The speed of the game, the intensity of the tackles and the sheer physical nature of the encounter with elbows, knees and fists flying in from all directions were all new to Paul. He left the field physically and mentally drained. As he trudged off the pitch towards the dressing rooms, he heard a shrill whistle from behind him. It came from kit man John Wilson, who beckoned him over with a wave of his hand. Pointing to Paul's scruffy brown football boots with nailed-in studs, Wilson, who was nicknamed "Whippet" because of his small, wiry build, growled: "You'll have to get rid of those boots, lad, if you want to play Rugby League. They're no good for this game. You need to wear them tighter than that!"

Paul was taken aback, but before training the following Tuesday, he walked around to Bernie Yates's sports shop in Roper Street, Whitehaven, and bought a new pair of size eight boots. When he arrived at training, John inspected the new footwear, before pointing Paul in the direction of the bath, where he was ordered to stand with the boots immersed in water for 20 minutes while they moulded to the exact shape of his feet. Now those boots were made for playing Rugby League.

★ ★ ★

Competition for places at Derwent Park was fierce as dozens of young players dreamed of pulling on a Workington jersey. Paul had not fully realised what he was up against until he received a shock ultimatum.

"You've got three more games. If you don't shape up, I'm afraid we're going to have to let you go."

Billy Miller's no-nonsense warning hit where it hurt. It was short, straight to the point and enough to leave Paul devastated. In six short weeks and as many games he had gone from feeling on top of the world to utter despair. But Paul knew there was only one way to stop his dreams crashing so soon at only 19-years-old. He had to dedicate his life to Rugby League.

That Saturday, Town were playing Oldham in the Lancashire

Combination League. Paul was even more determined then usual and came up with a new game plan to make him stand out. Taking full advantage of his fitness and speed, he altered his style of play to become an attacking full-back. It made him a more rounded and versatile player and was later to transform him into the greatest full-back of his generation.

DEBUT BOY

IT was the start of the Swinging Sixties, the era of mini-skirts, VW Beetles and the baby boom. The Everley Brothers were riding high in the hit parade with *Cathy's Clown*, along with Roy Orbison's *Only The Lonely*. At the cinema, Tony Curtis and Debbie Reynolds teamed up for the first time in *The Rat Race* and John Wayne, Richard Widmark and Laurence Harvey starred in the latest Western *The Alamo*. Prime Minister Harold MacMillan, addressing the Commonwealth Parliamentary Conference at Westminster Hall, London, summed up the mood of the era when he said: "We live in a strange world – poised between hope and despair".

Russia had just announced it would resume testing nuclear weapons and warned the West that rockets similar to those used by cosmonauts Gagarin and Titov could wing the new super-powerful bombs to any part of the world. Locally, the Independent Television Authority announced it would start to transmit TV programmes on a new channel to be known as Border TV, from new studios at Harraby, Carlisle.

Many of the happenings in the outside world passed by virtually unheard of in the close-knit community of Whitehaven. Josephine Charlton, as usual, was sitting impatiently waiting for the weekly home delivery service of Lowden's meat van. Every week she would buy her Sunday joint from Lowden's, who owned a butcher's shop in Hensingham. Their son Syd was a team-mate of Paul's at Workington. He was first choice full-back, after taking over the jersey from Jock McAvoy. The blue and white van eventually pulled up on Fell View Avenue and Syd sounded the horn to alert the customers.

"Is Paul in, Mrs Charlton? I could do with a quick word with him," said Syd.

Josephine popped her head back into the house and called her son outside.

"It looks like you could be in the team to face Rochdale on Saturday. I'm still struggling with this leg injury", Syd told him.

The following night after training, Billy Ivison pinned the team sheet on the notice board outside the dressing room. Pencilled in at number one was the name P. Charlton. The match was away at Rochdale Hornets on September 23, 1961 and the team was virtually at full strength apart from the absent Lowden. Town had made an impressive start to the new campaign and were unbeaten in their opening games.

Paul sat in the dressing room in nervous anticipation, convinced his team-mates could hear his heart beating loudly in his chest and sense his anxiety. Kick-off was looming and the players had returned from their warm-up on the pitch to strap up and rub themselves in Vaseline. The noise of studs clattering on the hard floor pierced the eerie silence which had descended on the dressing room as the players psyched themselves up for the game. Ike Southward put a reassuring hand on Paul's shoulder.

"If you weren't good enough, you wouldn't be in the team", he told him quietly.

Rochdale's Athletic Ground was a happy hunting ground for Workington. The last six meetings between the two sides had resulted in Town victories. And so it was to prove again, despite a below-par performance by Ivison's men, who ground out a 14-4 victory in the driving rain in front of a crowd of 2,000.

The match report in the Workington *Times & Star* spoke about the young Charlton in glowing terms.

"One encouraging fact to emerge from the game was the sound performance of 19-year-old ex-Kells full-back Paul Charlton, playing in his first senior game. His catching of the slippery ball was immaculate and he never panicked when in an awkward position".

"Owing to the excellence of the Town defence, his tackling ability was not put to the fullest test, and the only phase of the play in which the injured Lowden was missed was in attack."

The teams that day were: Rochdale: Pritchard, Lawrenson, Atherton, Evans, Unsworth, Dickinson, Hilton, McFarlane, Lea, Parr, Thomas, Pugsley, McGurrin.

Workington Town: Charlton, Southward, O'Neil, Ferreira, Pretorius, Archer, Roper, Herbert, Eden, Martin, Edgar, McLeod, Eve.

Referee: L. Wingfield (Normanton).

★ ★ ★

Dedication and determination were the hallmarks of Paul Charlton's career. Both attributes were in evidence right from the beginning. He was driven by a focused determination even though he was always dogged by a fear of failure and a nagging self-doubt that he was good enough to achieve his goals. His sights were set firmly on making the full-back position his own at Derwent Park and representing both Cumberland and Great Britain.

He knew he could not rely on talent alone and worked painstakingly hard at developing his pace and fitness to give him the edge over opponents, often man mountains, whose huge physical presence would dwarf his 5'10", twelve-and-a-half stone frame. After passing his driving test, he bought himself a pale blue Hillman Imp from Myers and Bowman in Distington, and after work would drive to St Bees. There he put himself through a gruelling training schedule, running along the beach and dunes or making the steep climb up St Bees Head. But before Paul could claim the number one jersey for himself he had to endure a long and frustrating three-year wait. During that time he made only a handful of appearances as deputy to first-choice full-back Syd Lowden. Like all young players, he suffered a roller-coaster ride of emotions as he staked his claim for a regular place in the side. He was to suffer many low points on his way to the top. With Lowden again on the sidelines injured, Paul was drafted into the side for a match at Wigan. It was not the only change Ivison made to the team. Another youngster, second row forward Rodney Smith, replaced the rested Danny Gardiner.

It was only Paul's second game in almost two years and he heaved a sigh of relief when he discovered Wigan's block-busting winger Billy Boston was ruled out with a chest injury. Wigan had already been beaten twice by Workington during the 1962-63 season, 16-8 in the Lancashire Cup on September 16 and 27-9 in the Western Division play-off on October 15. The game may not have stood out as a classic, but it marked Paul's first senior try. Wigan skipper Eric Ashton's grubber kick to the corner was picked up by Paul, who had only to drop over the line. Harry Archer's late 30-yard goal secured a remarkable hat-trick of victories for Town as they ran home 20-22 winners.

Paul was elated after playing a crucial part in Town's victory, but faced a nervous wait to discover whether he had done enough to persuade Ivison to keep him in the side at the expense of Lowden for the following week's game against Leeds. Then fate intervened and, with Southward being forced to miss the game with a pulled muscle, Lowden was brought back in on the left-wing. Paul retained his place at full-back. It was his Derwent Park debut in front of his family and friends and 4,120 other fans. In a hard-fought game, Paul emerged as one of the heroes. *The Sunday People* reported: "Charlton not only turned in a steady game, but settled down well enough, and with loads of confidence, to sally forth on a number of raids into Leeds territory long before Workington made certain of success".

★ ★ ★

The news from Whitehaven Hospital was much better. John and Violet Wilson had visited Paul as they had promised to give him news of their daughter Lily.

Paul and Lily had been going out together for just over a year, although they had been friends much longer after meeting at Mirehouse Youth Club, where he played table tennis. Seventeen-year-old Lily, from Mirehouse, worked at Millers Shoe Factory in Egremont. She hadn't been in good health for a few months, although the doctors struggled to decide what was wrong.

A series of tests at Whitehaven Hospital revealed kidney disease. Doctors informed the family of their intention to remove the infected organ. For several weeks Lily struggled to survive. The worry hung like a cloud over Paul, who had been devastated by his sweetheart's illness. The words of John and Violet lifted him from his gloom. Lily was off the critical list and would make a full recovery.

ONE FOR THE FUTURE

THE vows had been made, the speeches were over and the wedding party was in full swing. But there was one notable absentee – the bridegroom. Paul had kissed Lillian goodbye after the champagne reception and headed for Derwent Park. It may have been his wedding day but it was also an important day for Workington, who had a vital home clash with Barrow that afternoon.

It was January 2, 1965. Paul and Lillian had tied the knot at 11am at St Mary's Church in Kells, before a reception at Woolsten Hall in Duke Street, Whitehaven. Paul was now an important member of the Workington side. Nothing could stand in the way of Rugby League, not even his wedding. While Lillian and their guests stayed to celebrate, Paul and team-mates Spanky McFarlane and David Curwen set off for the game. It was a day when nothing could go wrong for Paul. He scored a try as Workington secured a 20-6 victory over their North-West rivals in front of a crowd of nearly 3,000. Later that afternoon, Paul was reunited with his new bride and the couple left for their honeymoon in Edinburgh.

Paul ended the 1964-65 season with 40 appearances under his belt. He had also scored 11 tries, his best haul to date. The season had seen a return to the old one division set-up and Workington enhanced their reputation as one of the most powerful teams in Rugby League, winning 23 of their 34 fixtures. Against his former club Oldham on October 17, the evergreen Ike Southward extended his own career points for the club to more than 1,000.

Another well-established star, Brian Edgar made a landmark 300th appearance on February 13 in the home game with St Helens, while Harry Archer completed 350 appearances on April 19 at home to Huddersfield.

At 23, Paul was still the baby of the side but he was already carving out a considerable reputation for himself. He was a fearless competitor, strong enough to take on the might of 16-stone opponents running at him like steamrollers and capable of shrugging off the knocks. Meanwhile, his pace, power and eye for the try-line had caught the attention of the Cumberland selectors. Cumberland were handed the sternest of tests in their opening county championship match of the season when they travelled to Hull K.R's Craven Park to face title holders Yorkshire on September 8, 1965. Paul was joined in the side by five of his Workington team-mates, Tony Colloby, Eric Bell, Bill Smith,

Brian Edgar and Spanky McFarlane.

In spite of torrential rain, which left the pitch resembling a swimming pool, the crowd of 4,500 were treated to an entertaining spectacle. Paul could not have asked for a tougher game to make his debut. He passed the test of his ability with flying colours. Along with Whitehaven stand-off Phil Kitchin, he turned in a fine display as the Cumberland backs took the honours in the game.

The match was not only the first county championship game of the season. For about half the players on the pitch, it represented the first step up the gangway of the plane which would depart for the tour of a lifetime to Australia. The places in the British Test side, not to mention the 26-man squad required for the tour, were still wide open. Paul hadn't realised that Great Britain selectors were in the crowd, and his name had been noted as one for the future.

★ ★ ★

Paul gazed out of the window. It had been threatening rain all morning, but the dark clouds had finally started to clear and it was looking brighter. It was his day off work. He badly needed it. The previous night he had been part of the Cumberland team which had beaten Lancashire 14-11 at the Recreation Ground to be crowned county champions. It had been a tough game. He had paid the price for a good performance and needed a day to recover from the inevitable knocks.

Paul was still working as a carpenter for Border Engineers, helping to construct the Pearl Insurance office in Lowther Street, Whitehaven. But he had managed to get a rest day and planned to have a relaxing time fishing on Parton beach. It was a rewarding trip and he returned home with his catch in a box. As he pulled up outside his house in Copeland Avenue, Mirehouse, he could see his father waiting at the front door with an anxious look on his face.

"Where on earth have you been?" said Harold. "The club's desperately been trying to find you. You've been picked for Great Britain."

Jimmy Hodgson, the Town secretary had been given the shock news of Paul's selection for the game against New Zealand at Odsal on October 23, 1965, by Rugby League secretary Bill Fallowfield. Paul had been selected for the Great Britain shadow squad 10 days earlier but Swinton's Kenny Gowers had been picked as first choice full-back, only to withdraw from the squad through injury. Hodgson had hurried over to Paul's to pass on the news. When he found the house empty he had dashed around to see Harold and Josephine.

Paul hurriedly packed his suitcase. There were only two days to go before the big game and he had to get to Bradford quickly.

★ ★ ★

New Zealand embarked on their English tour on August 13 leaving Auckland by Canadian Pacific Airways. Test results from the previous two years pointed to Australia as the leading nation, but it was the Kiwis who held the Courtney Goodwill Trophy, the symbol of world Rugby League supremacy. The selectors had sprung one or two surprises for the 1965 tour. The squad contained a useful blend of youth and experience. It included seven new players. They were centres Leo Brown and Robin Strong, second-row Bill Deacon, half-back Bob Irvine, stand-off John Walshe, winger Pat White and second-row Robin Orchard who, at 19, was the youngest player in the party. The squad contained the best set of hookers ever to be sent to England in Colin O'Neil and Bill Schultz. They were expected to get their fair share of possession from the scrums. It also boasted the power and experience of Graham Kennedy and Roger Bailey at centre, solid props Maunga Emery, Sam Edwards and Eddie Moore and lively ball-playing forwards Graham Mattson and Kevin Dixon.

Tries by Britain's Bill Burgess, Geoff Shelton and John Stopford and three goals from Bill Holliday earned them a 15-9 win and the Test series, but it was a hollow victory. In a frustrating afternoon for the 15,740 supporters who had turned up expecting to see an exciting display, the game failed to live up to New Zealand's pre-tour hype. The tourists were lacklustre and tactically flawed, while Britain did little to convince fans that they were capable of bringing the Ashes home from Australia the following year. There were two basic weaknesses in the British side, a failure to win the ball in scrums and the absence of an accurate goal-kicker.

The English press could find little to enthuse about, but Roland Tinker in the *Halifax Courier* said: "There was nothing wrong with the display of newcomer Paul Charlton at full-back".

Eddie Waring, writing in the *Sunday Mirror*, picked out Paul as one for the future. "Charlton will be a lot better for the experience", he wrote.

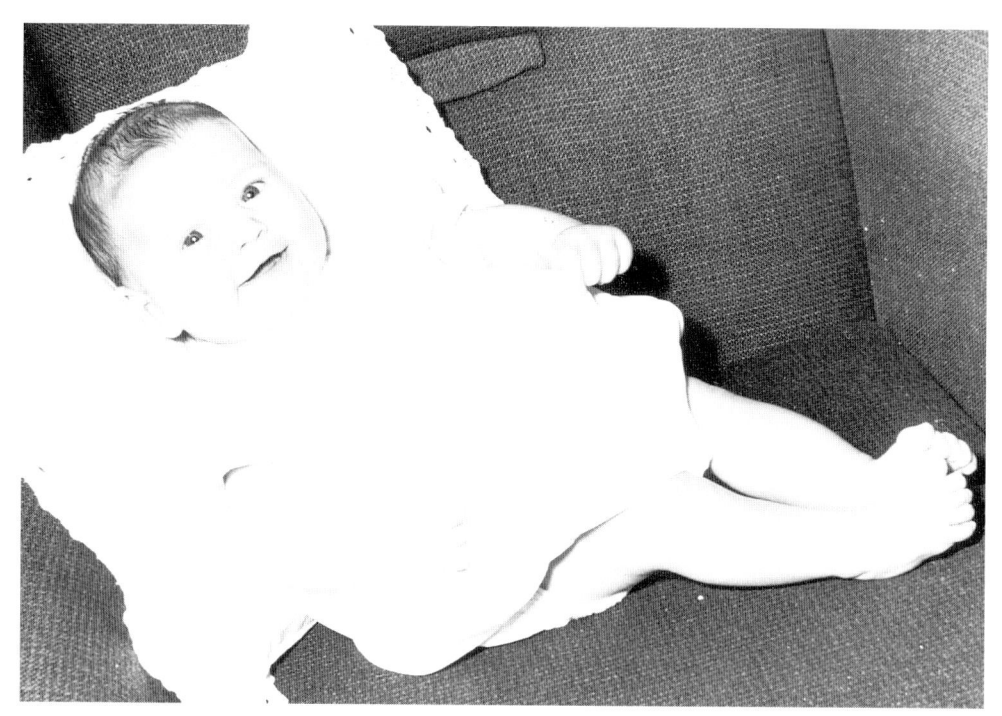

Paul as a baby. He was born on December 6, 1941 at the family's home on Woodhouse estate, Whitehaven, the oldest of Josephine and Harold Charlton's four children.

The Charlton family pictured outside their home in Coach Road, where they moved to shortly after Paul's birth. Josephine is holding three-year-old Paul and Harold is holding his sister Jean, 15 months younger.

Paul aged seven. He attended St Mary's Junior School in Kells and was already beginning to show an interest in Rugby League. His grandfather Robert Charlton was a Whitehaven fan and took his grandson to matches.

Paul as a teenager on holiday at Butlins in Ayr in 1958. Left to right: Brothers Tom and Joe Walker, Raymond "Gosh" Reeves and Paul. Paul was working at Whitehaven Brick Works and playing for Kells Under-19s.

Jim and Madge Kitchen, two leading lights behind the hugely-successful Kells amateur team. Jim, an overman at Haig Pit, ran the administration side from his living room, while Madge was both treasurer and laundry woman.

Henry Brown, the Kells full-back, who won England amateur honours. He watched Paul as a teenager playing on the field behind Fell View Avenue and predicted he would play for Great Britain. Ten years later at Odsal, Bradford, his prophecy came true.

Kells Under-19s in 1958-59. Back (left to right): Ralph Watson, Alan Garret, Alan O'Fee, Geoff Sewell, Eddie Brennan, Michael McFarlane, John Thompson, Vince Corkhill. Front: Les Herbert, John Kirkbride, Alan King, Watson Lightfoot, Phil Kitchin, Raymond Douglas, Roland Johnstone, Paul Charlton, Billy Vaughan. The team won the County Championship and the Lockhart Trophy.

Kells Under-19s in 1959-60. Back (left to right): Jackie Brennan, Duncan Walker, Derek Rea, Pop Philips, John Gaskill, Gilbert Martin, Matt Coward, Michael McFarlane, Jim Kitchen, Watson Lightfoot, Billy Gainford. Middle: Kenny Sloane, Raymond Johnstone, John Davidson, Paul Charlton, John Thompson, Paul Peadersen, Ernie Rea, William Proud. Front: William Pickering, Joe Scott, Geoff Sewell, John McFarlane, Raymond Douglas, Algie Adams, Matt Black, Tom Wren. Mascot: Boxer Walker. The team won the Under-19 County Championship, the Cumberland Shield, the Whitehaven & District Trophy and the Billy Farrer Memorial Trophy.

Workington Town's inspirational coach Billy Ivison. The Prince among Forwards played for Great Britain and Workington. He handed Paul his debut against Rochdale on September 23, 1961.

Workington Town's late president Tom Mitchell, who developed a close bond with Paul. He describes the day Paul was sold to Salford as one of his saddest.

Billy Ivison announcing his team before a match. Left to right: John O'Neil, Billy Ivison, Paul, Ike Southward, Ray Glastonbury, Harry Archer. Billy Martin is lying on the treatment table.

Workington star Syd Lowden was Paul's rival for the full-back shirt.

Tony Colloby was Paul's team-mate at Town and Salford.

Huge prop Brian Edgar, gentle off the field but a hard man on it.

Harry Archer was a Great Britain tourist in 1958.

The Cumberland team which won the County Championship in the early 1960s receive their medals from the mayor and mayoress. Left to right: Brian Edgar, Paul Charlton, Billy Smith, Eric Bell, John McFarlane, Tony Colloby, Harry Archer, Ike Southward.

Paul in derby action for Workington against Whitehaven, the home-town club he always dreamed of joining.

Paul in full flight against Swinton in one of ten appearances he made for Workington in 1962-63 as he tried to dislodge Syd Lowden from the number one shirt.

Workington Town line up for the cameras in 1963. Back (left to right): Danny Gardner, Billy Martin, Walter Tabburn, David Curwen, Rodney Smith, Spanky McFarlane, Ike Southward. Front: Harry Hughes, Tom McNally, Paul Charlton, Jacky Newall, Harry Archer, Eric Bell.

Paul and Lillian marry at St Mary's Church in Kells on January 2, 1965. Four hours later Paul was in action for Workington against Barrow, and scored a try in his side's 20-6 victory.

THE BIG TIME BECKONS

THE footsteps coming down the garden path of Paul's home in Copeland Avenue, Mirehouse, sounded familiar. They were followed by the sharp rap of the letterbox as the paper lad dropped the morning newspaper onto the doormat. Paul turned straight to the sports pages as he walked back to the breakfast table, where Lillian was feeding their toddler son Gary, born two years earlier. As he scanned the pages of Rugby League news there was his own face staring back at him from the *Daily Express* under the banner headline SALFORD WANT WORKINGTON STAR CHARLO.

The story revealed that Salford's ambitious chairman Brian Snape had made a bid for him, which had been turned down by Workington. It was the first Paul had heard of Salford's interest but deep down he desperately hoped every word was true and not just paper talk. He felt stuck in a rut at Derwent Park. It was almost four years to the day since he had made his Great Britain debut. Ever since then there had been a deafening silence from the selectors. The disappointment of being left out of the 1966 Tour of Australia had been painful. Time was now running out for him to earn his selection for the 1970 Tour Down Under. He was being kept out of the Great Britain side by Hull full-back Arthur Keegan, and could see no way back into the Test side unless he moved on to a higher-profile club.

Paul was still ambitious, and was beginning to despair that he would never be given another international chance. Workington were in decline and, at 28, he couldn't afford another season with a club in the shadow of the big guns.

Paul made his 200th appearance for Workington in a 13-2 defeat against St Helens on October 19, 1968. He appeared in all of Town's 40 fixtures that season – the first player to do so since Gus Risman in 1953-54. Paul also came close to claiming another record when, on April 19, 1969, he scored 26 points – four tries and seven goals – in a 38-10 victory at home to Warrington. His tally made him Town's second highest points scorer, only seven short of the record set by his close friend Ike Southward in the 1955-56 season.

One of Paul's tries was the longest individual effort ever seen at Derwent Park. He collected the ball behind his own try line at the Town end of the ground close to the popular side corner flag. He turned to meet the on-coming Warrington players and cut diagonally across the field, before straightening up and going through the defenders as if they didn't exist. The following season got off to a bad start for Workington with a humiliating opening day derby defeat against Whitehaven. Town went down 18-13 in a game in which Paul kicked two goals. A week later they were dumped out of the Lancashire Cup at Widnes, where they lost 16-15, despite the fact that the home side scored only two tries to Town's three, including one from Paul.

Many of the club's stalwarts had moved on or retired and there was speculation that more would be on their way. The decline in Town's fortunes had been sudden, and the disappointment on the pitch was inevitably reflected in the number of fans going through the turnstiles. Neighbours Whitehaven were closely monitoring the situation, and coach Ron Morgan had Charlton at the top of his shopping list. Morgan was realistic enough to realise they would not be able to compete for Paul's signature with a club like Salford. Workington would also make sure he was not sold cheaply. This was displayed three years earlier when Paul, disillusioned at a lack of first team opportunities, had presented the chairman Jim Graves with a written transfer request after he was left out of the side in favour of Syd Lowden. Workington responded by putting a hefty £11,000 transfer fee on his head, a record for the club.

But that fee did not deter Salford. They were a progressive, go-ahead club being transformed by millionaire Brian Snape. The wealthy entrepreneur, who was involved in restaurants and cinemas, was happy to buy success. He wanted big names at his club and had the financial clout to recruit them. Snape and coach Cliff Evans had been impressed with Charlton's performance when Salford met Workington earlier in the season. His pace and skills would be an exciting addition to the squad and Snape was not a man to take No for an answer, even though he had received one knock-back from Workington.

"This boy is a superb player with great attacking ability and the best defence I have ever seen from a full-back", Snape told the newspapers. "I've been after him for a long time but my mind was made up when I saw how he managed to send David Watkins the way he wanted, then picked him off with crashing tackles.

"No other full-back could have done this and they were the highlights of our last game with Workington, even though they cost us the chance of winning."

Paul knew the only way to revive his international ambitions was to leave for a bigger club. Salford was just the kind of dream move he was looking for, but it was out of his hands and he would just have to sit back and wait for developments. He folded the newspaper, tucked it into his haversack with his bait box and set off for another day on the building site.

★ ★ ★

If you said it quickly, £12,500 didn't sound much, Paul thought to himself. Salford had upped the pressure on the Town board to part with their prized asset and had agreed to pay a world record transfer fee for a full-back. It was easy for players to blame poor performances on the pressure placed upon them by big fees, but Paul was determined not to be daunted by it.

The move to Salford not only made him the world's costliest full-back, it also introduced him to a different way of life. The £1,000 he received as his share of the £12,500 transfer deal was his first taste of real financial success in a game he had served loyally for eight years. From his first two games in three days he collected £50 in wages, compared with the £14 winning bonus received at Workington.

By day, Paul could still be found on a building site overshadowed by the floodlights of Old Trafford, where another Charlton earned £15,000 a year as a footballer. Bobby and his Manchester United team-mates were regular visitors to Salford, where the home games were played on a Friday evening to avoid a clash with their footballing neighbours. The soccer players at Old Trafford enjoyed the kind of status usually reserved for pop groups and film stars. Names like Charlton, Best and Law were famous all over the world.

While Salford's Rugby League players may have lived in the shadows of their illustrious neighbours, Friday nights at The Willows always promised to be something special. The Salford players may have been stars on the pitch but they didn't behave that way off it. There were no prima donnas, just down-to-earth Rugby League players paid to do a job they loved. Team spirit was one of their greatest strengths.

Salford had thought and bought big in the last few seasons. Halifax second-rower Colin Dixon, Castleford prop Johnny Ward, Swinton prop Peter Smethurst, and England Rugby Union international Mike Coulman, from Moseley, were added to the team. David Watkins, one of Rugby Union's most celebrated players and a former captain of Wales, joined the club in 1967. In the 15-man game, the diminutive fly-half won 21 Welsh caps and toured Australasia with the 1966 British Lions, skippering them in two Tests against New Zealand. Paul was surrounded by class players who could quickly read a game, making it easy for him to slot into the team when he made his debut in Salford's victory over St Helens on October 29, 1969.

Paul, Lillian and Gary moved into a flat above Brian Snape's offices in Kildare Road. Five months later they moved from their temporary home into a club house. Paul's transfer to Salford only added to the dissatisfaction of Workington supporters, enraged that one of their few class players had been sold. The club was in turmoil and many fans vowed not to return until the board began to show the same ambition Salford had demonstrated.

A GROWING REPUTATION

PAUL began his first full season at The Willows in sparkling form. His reputation was spreading far and wide, from Odsal to Central Park to Headingley and Knowsley Road. His toughness and determination as a competitor were tempered by modesty and a lack of pretentiousness, which evoked warmth and admiration from supporters and team-mates alike. Confidence burned inside him as the number of man-of-the-match accolades grew steadily as reward for his try-scoring exploits and crash-tackling in defence. Paul was revelling in the new spotlight.

The start of the 1970-71 season also saw him earn his 12th Cumberland cap when he played in his home county's 21-15 victory over Yorkshire at Whitehaven. Despite the rave reviews in the press and adulation from Salford fans, Paul's career was not going the way he wanted. It had been five frustrating years since his Great Britain debut against New Zealand. The experience was beginning to feel like a distant memory and, at 28, he was beginning to despair that he would never again don a red, white and blue shirt. His exploits on the pitch for club and county had again been met by a baffling silence from the Great Britain selectors.

It was no consolation that his path into the international team was blocked by some of the finest full-backs in the game. Hull's Arthur Keegan, Ken Gowers, of Swinton, Bev Risman, of Leeds, Ray Dutton, of Widnes and Castleford's Dereck Edwards seemed to form a brick wall between Paul and his dream of international recognition.

He had been disappointed not to be selected for the 1970 Tour of Australia. Bradford Northern's Welsh full-back Terry Price had played in the first Test, kicking three goals in their 37-15 defeat. Edwards had replaced him in the second match, a 28-7 victory for the Lions, while Leeds' Mick Shoebottom filled the position in the third and final game, which saw Britain clinch the Ashes with a 21-17 victory. Paul felt powerless. He was playing his heart out, week in week out, but still the selectors overlooked him. It was out of his hands and all he could do was concentrate his efforts on helping spearhead Salford's push for the title and hope one day his chance of playing for Great Britain again would come.

★ ★ ★

After the triumphant 1970 tour of Australia, it was the countdown to the World Cup series.

The Salford City Reporter's Rugby League columnist Tom Bergin wrote: "As a returned tourist and goal-kicker, Ray Dutton possibly has the edge with the selectors, but in my opinion Paul is the outstanding full-back in the game, especially now that he is back to his attacking best and among the tries.

"Paul would dearly like to break Colin Tyrer's record of 21 tries with Wigan and on his current form he should do so."

Bergin was proved right when the squad was announced. Dutton was named as full-back and Paul, who had hardly dared hope he would be included, was pencilled in as a squad member. After five long years in the international wilderness, he was named as a substitute for the third game against New Zealand at Swinton. He replaced Keith Hepworth after 67 minutes and Great Britain went on to beat the Kiwis 27-17 in convincing fashion.

★ ★ ★

Football had boasted Jack and Bobby but now Rugby League was about to have its answer to the Charlton brothers. The question everyone was asking was would Philip turn out to be as good as Paul?

Whitehaven, who had missed out on Paul's signature, made sure they captured the younger Charlton from the amateur game. Only a week after making his debut for Egremont Rangers in the Cumberland Amateur Rugby League, Philip signed for the professional club. He had caught their eye with two tries in Egremont's match with Glasson, one of which was a breathtaking 75-yarder.

Unlike Paul, Philip, seven years younger, stood almost 6ft 2in and weighed almost 13 stone. But like his more famous brother he could side-step his opponents and show them a clean pair of heels. He was a late-starter in the professional game and, while he was not expected to hit the same heights as his brother, Philip was about to carve out an equally satisfying career of his own.

Also back in Whitehaven, Lillian had returned briefly to Cumbria to give birth to the couple's second child, a daughter called Melanie, at the West Cumberland Hospital on February 10, 1971. At last, their family was complete.

★ ★ ★

Salford's trophy cabinet had been under lock and key for almost four decades. There had never been any need to open it. The Reds had not won a major trophy for 34 years. During the Thirties Salford had dominated the Lancashire Cup, winning it three seasons on the trot with victories over Wigan in 1934-35, 1935-36 and 1936-37. They had not reached the final since 1938 when Wigan had at last exacted their revenge by beating them 10-7 at Swinton. After a long lean spell, their fortunes changed in 1972 when they reached the final against Swinton at Warrington.

The omens were not good for Salford who went into the game without star forwards Mike Coulman, Terry Ramshaw and Billy Kirkbride. Meanwhile, their new £13,500 pack star Eric Prescott was playing his first game after a three-week absence through injury. As things turned out, the Salford fans' 34-year wait for glory was rewarded with a 25-11 victory against a gritty Swinton side. And when the final whistle blew, on the scoresheet was a certain P. Charlton. Prop forward Johnny Ward's ability to commit Swinton's defenders to the tackle while still managing to get the ball to supporting attackers was a key feature of Salford's performance. Ward was well supported by foraging runs from Stuart Whitehead and Graham Mackay and, with their forwards in outstanding form, the backs were not slow to capitalise. Kenny Gill and Peter Banner were in fine form, while Chris Hesketh and David Watkins, so often the stars of the big occasions, were dominant in the centres.

Paul turned in a fine all-round display at full-back and weighed in with his impressive try. It was characteristic of Paul's attacking play. He took a pass from Hesketh 60 yards out and went on a diagonal run, leaving Swinton winger Bobby Fleay trailing in his wake. But Fleay kept up the chase, pushing Paul all the way to the try-line, until he could place the ball over the line and raise his arm in jubilation. Ward summed up the Salford feelings when he said: "We needed this win badly. Perhaps we can now forget our inferiority complex and win some more".

Teams:

Salford: Charlton, Eastham, Watkins, Hesketh, Richards, Gill, Banner, Mackay, Walker, Ward, Whitehead, Dixon, Prescott, subs: Orr and Davies.

Swinton: Jackson, Fleay, Cooke, Buckley, Gomersall, Kenny (Philbin), Gowers, Halsall, Evans, Bate, Smith (Holliday), Hoyle, Pattinson.

Referee: W. H. Thompson (Huddersfield).

THE WORLD IN HIS HANDS

GREAT Britain's countdown towards the 1972 World Cup in France began with two games against the host nation early in the year. Britain were to send a team to Toulouse in February, before entertaining the French at Bradford's Odsal Stadium the following month. Paul was thrilled to be named in the team, which would fly out to France for the first encounter on February 6. Selectors were bound to use both games to try out players for the World Cup. Paul had been desperate to have his chance to impress but after the disappointment of being left out of the 1970 squad which toured Australia, he decided not to waste any time torturing himself with pointless speculation. He had been in fine form for Salford, but he was aware there were several other full-backs with legitimate claims for selection for the World Cup.

Castleford's Dereck Edwards had been part of the Great Britain squad which toured Australia in 1970. Reports in the press indicated he was likely to keep his place. But injury had forced him to withdraw from the game in Toulouse, and opened the way for Paul. The pressure was on. He knew any mistakes would destroy his World Cup prospects. Any thoughts of his dynamic, attacking style were suppressed and Paul opted to play a careful, controlled game where he would be less likely to make mistakes. His usual style with Salford was an expansive game, going out wide and taking players on. He was determined he would take the safer option of sacrificing personal glory if the chance came to set up another player for a try.

Great Britain won 10-9 and, as the scoreline suggested, it was touch and go. More importantly for Paul, his game plan worked. He retained the full-back's shirt for the return match on March 12 at Bradford. His inclusion in the side for the second game was a huge vote of confidence and it showed in his performance in Britain's convincing 45-10 victory. He was more relaxed and composed and he capped an impressive individual performance with his first international try. It came from a simple passing move which saw Paul take a pass out wide before scoring a text-book try in the corner.

Paul had much to celebrate that night when he returned home to Salford. An impressive victory by the team and a confident performance from himself left him feeling on cloud nine. All he had to do was sit and wait to see if the selectors had been sufficiently impressed to pick him for that autumn's World Cup in France.

Although he suffered waves of doubt, unknown to Paul, his goal had already been achieved.

★ ★ ★

The players piled onto the British Airways plane bound for Toulouse. Excited chatter and laughter filled the plane as it taxied up the runway and the players cheered as it soared into the air. They were on their way to do battle for Britain in the World Cup. They were men on a mission with a big point to prove. Back home, their chances of lifting the World Cup for the first time since 1960 had been written off. Skipper Clive Sullivan and his team had been dismissed as no-hopers. But this lack of support succeeded only in motivating them further. They were more determined than ever to prove their critics wrong.

The Great Britain squad assembled under St Helens coach Jim Challinor was radically different from the outfit which had returned victorious from the 1970 Tour of Australia. While the team may have been derided back home, other nations refused to under-estimate them. Australian coach Harry Bath, the former Warrington player, summed up the task facing his side when he said: "The team we have to beat are the Poms".

During the flight Paul was relaxing with his Salford team-mate Chris Hesketh on one side and Dewsbury's Mike Stephenson on the other. The talk was inevitably about the stiff task ahead of the them against Australia, New Zealand and France. After landing at Toulouse, the players were taken to their hotel at Perpignon. There, they spent the evening relaxing before the next day's game against Australia on October 29. They could not have asked for a harder game to start the tournament. Paul was not a drinker, but he decided to sample some of the French beers the other players were buying at the bar. They were allowed a couple of pints just to help them unwind and take away the tension.

Paul, who rarely drank anything stronger than coke or orange squash, had three pints of lager, before heading off to the room he was sharing with Chris Hesketh. But Paul hadn't bargained for the potency of the French beer. Although he went to bed totally sober, the next morning he woke up with the worst hang over he had experienced. The room around him seemed to be spinning, making his head reel and he could feel himself breaking into a cold sweat. Quickly, he sprang out of bed and ran to the bathroom to be violently sick.

By lunch time, he had still not managed to make it out of his bed, apart from several more trips to the bathroom. He was in despair. Here he was, about to represent his country in a major tournament. Were those years of hard work and sacrifice about to be shattered because of three lousy bottles of beer? Kick-off was only hours away, and he was determined his condition was not going to cost him his place in the team. By 1.30pm, he was on the coach with the rest of the squad heading for the match.

As the players began changing into their international strips, the stench of lineament filled Paul's lungs and he could feel himself becoming queasy again. He walked out on to the pitch to warm up, taking deep breaths of air to clear his aching head and help him focus on the game. Australia were led out by their 6ft, 13st captain Graeme Langlands, an awesome talent, who was at his best when the going got tough. Even bigger than Langlands was Artie Beetson, who stood at 6ft 2in and weighed in at over 16st. The huge prop had the strength to match his size, and he put it to good use on the field. He was a player who was not afraid of confrontation. The crowd loved him for it. The strains of *God Save The Queen* were almost lost on Paul as he stood alongside the huge, intimidating brutes towering over him in the famous green and gold of Australia, feeling small and innocuous in comparison. By the time the whistle went, he was perspiring with anticipation. His heart pounded in his chest as the game kicked off and he felt considerably ill.

After the worst possible build-up for a game of such importance, Paul handled the occasion remarkably well, and played a vital role in Britain's unexpected 27-21 victory. Australia, after boasting they had the biggest and fittest team in the world, had proved no match on football ability. On top of that, their fearsome pack was tamed. Paul was involved in two crucial incidents which contributed to Australia's downfall. The first came when Australia's giant 16-and-a-half stone winger Mark Harris made a dangerous break with only Paul to beat. At the sight of the Great Britain full-back's compact frame he charged forward like a runaway train. It was a David and Goliath contest, the kind of challenge Paul thrived on. Like David, Paul decided it was not a case of his opponent being too big to hit, simply too big to miss. He shut his eyes and steeled himself, before diving headlong and grabbing Harris around the ankles, cutting him down in full flight.

Bobby Fulton provided Paul with another chance to prove that his attacking sorties could be matched by some equally impressive defensive play. His speed allowed him to cut down the quickest wingers, and he had the ability to shepherd ball-carriers where he wanted them. Fulton powered his way towards the try-line with a 40-

yard run with Paul close behind. Paul managed to grab his shirt, before Clive Sullivan came over in support with a try-saving tackle.

After the match Paul won the praise of Australian coach Harry Bath, who acknowledged his impact on the game. Great Britain Tour manager Wilf Spavin summed up the match when he told reporters that his players had displayed a "great show of guts and ability".

Coach Jim Challinor said: "Football won the game, and I was glad the referee gave us a fair deal. The main thing was that the lads proved to themselves that they could match Australia".

Hooker Mike Stephenson, who won the scrums 18-17, said: "They tried to steam-roller us but it didn't work".

Hesketh added: "Punches were going in and the boot as well. Games don't come any tougher than this".

★ ★ ★

After the thrill of beating the Kangaroos, Great Britain turned their attentions to the dark horses of the tournament, the host nation France. But, in contrast to their triumph over Australia, Britain failed to reach great heights at the Alpin Ground in Grenoble. Nevertheless, a workmanlike performance saw them run in three tries to win 13-4. The celebrations in the British dressing room were kept to a minimum. They all knew they had got away with a sub-standard performance. After the gruelling encounter with Australia, most of the British players were looking for an easy passage, and France were never good enough to test their opponents to the full.

Had the host nation reaped a richer dividend from the seven penalties they received to Britain's four, the 4,500 crowd might have enjoyed a better spectacle. Only two penalty goals resulted from seven attempts and the French lacked the skill to score tries. The mood in the British camp was one of satisfaction rather than jubilation, but, as the only country unbeaten in the tournament, they had guaranteed themselves a place in the play-off between the two top teams.

First they faced New Zealand in Pau, a tough task, or so it seemed. In the event, Britain's performance against the Kiwis was superlative. They amazed the Rugby League world with their resounding 53-19 victory.

New Zealand's covering and tackling were slow and slipshod, their defence woefully weak. But this was a truly class performance by Britain to score 50 points against a southern hemisphere side It was Paul's best game so far at international level, which he capped with a try. Leeds star John Holmes replaced the injured Denis O'Neill at number six. He took his chance in impressive style, scoring two tries and kicking ten goals – an individual record in a World Cup match. Britain's total was also the highest by a British team in the competition or, for that matter, in any international match. Britain had not only beaten the New Zealanders, they had humbled them.

Afterwards Challinor told British reporters: "We played some tremendous football and made the ball do the work. "Every man was running onto the ball. Whenever we opened up we found a gap. The backing up was like watching the Harlem Globetrotters. It was harder than we made it look. We played like a really good club side."

★ ★ ★

Great Britain went into the final against Australia topping the World Cup table. An Australian side gunning for revenge were at their most dangerous. After their unexpected defeat by Britain, they had gone on to rout France 31-9. The scene was set for a cracking final. Britain were seeking their first World Cup success since 1960. Their opponents were hoping to complete a hat-trick of wins.

In a nervous opening, mistakes were commonplace, although neither side's cause was helped by a greasy pitch at the Gerland Stadium in Lyon. The Aussies seemed to get into their stride more quickly, and it took a good tackle from Paul to chop down Harris, who had been sent through after a clever back-pass by Bobby Fulton. At the back of everyone's mind was the unwelcome thought that no tie between Britain and Australia would ever be complete with the obligatory flare-up. This time it was sparked when British prop Terry Clawson, who had earlier put his side ahead with a towering 35-yard penalty goal, became involved in a brawl with three Australian players. At the same time Mike Stephenson was making a touchline run. He was penalised for a tackle on Graeme Langlands. O'Reilly took a wild swing at Jeanes without being penalised. All hell broke loose. The mayhem knocked Britain out of their stride and the defence stood rooted as O'Neill ran from midfield in a 30-yard arc to score in the corner. Branighan added the conversion.

The British handling was not yet up to standard and they were lucky to escape further punishment by the Australians. Clive Sullivan restored Britain's confidence and brought the French crowd to their feet with a fine try after a 70-yard run up the wing. The game was stalemate at half-time. It was to remain that way at full-time with the score at 10-10.

A draw would secure the cup for Britain because of their superior scoring average. But could Challinor's men have the strength and stamina to survive extra time after an 80 minute battering at the hands of the Aussies? The atmosphere could have been cut with a knife as Britain almost put the tie beyond doubt when Clawson kicked at goal. His shot was just wide. The tension mounted in the second period of extra-time as Australia turned to their forwards in a late bid for victory. But for the Aussies it was too late.

Britain's jubilation at the final whistle was clear to see. Players embraced each other and punched the air. Others sank to their knees in relief and exhaustion. The tired players trudged up the steps where their "Captain Marvel" Clive Sullivan received the cup, heads and backs patted and rubbed by the outstretched hands of supporters. Great Britain had provided the perfect response to their critics. They had come out of the World Cup as a major force in the game with their reputation enhanced. For Paul, it was the moment he had proved to the world he was the best full-back of his era. The attacking skills for which he was already renowned had survived the intense pressure of a massive stage. He had also displayed defensive qualities for which he had not previously been given credit.

Paul had handled the big occasion with incredible sang-froid, which belied his limited international experience. He looked proudly at the World Cup winner's medal held tightly in his hand as he drank in the euphoria of the occasion. It was a memory he would treasure for the rest of his life.

TRY, TRY, TRY AGAIN

THE full-back was traditionally looked upon as a player with the dual role of kicking goals and stopping tries. Gradually, however, a new style of full-back was emerging, bringing a new and exciting dimension to the game. Wigan's Martin Ryan had the pace, flair and strength to typify the new breed of adventurous full-back. He inspired a new generation to break out of the mould. Ryan's positional play and ability to sell a dummy meant he was the natural choice to represent Great Britain on two Australian tours in 1946 and 1950. The four-tackle rule began to inspire the men in the number one shirts to play an instrumental role in attack. One of Ryan's successors at Central Park also personified the changing role of the full-back. Colin Tyrer's try-scoring feats became something of a phenomenon. He scored on his debut following his transfer from Leigh in 1967 and in his first full season with Wigan set a new try scoring record for a full-back with 20 tries. As if to prove it was no fluke, he extended it by one the following season.

Paul also developed a reputation as one of the most talented full-backs of his era, although his style was not modelled on any other player. It had more to do with Paul himself. He had begun his career as a hooker because, at 5ft 10in and twelve-and-a-half stone, he was too small for the other positions. But as soon as he broke into the Workington first team he quickly learned he was going to have to adapt his game to cope with playing against mighty man-mountains who stood head and shoulders above him.

Some were 18 stone of intimidating brutality. They were hard men whose awesome physiques had been built up down the pit in the coalfields of Yorkshire, Lancashire and Cumberland, shifting huge amounts of coal in unimaginably foul conditions. Paul knew he would have to rely on his talent as an outstanding athlete rather than strength if he was to fulfil his dream of reaching the top. His team-mates nicknamed him "Road-Runner" after the cartoon character because of his speed and stamina.

The unquenchable ability to score tries rarely eluded him, but he was more than just an opportunist. His creativity and shrewd tactical sense helped him stand out, but the main weapon in his armoury was his speed. He had the turn of pace to take him beyond the reach of the best tacklers. These were all the qualities he needed to overcome the limitations of his physical frame.

Many players renowned as prolific try-scorers often drew a veil over their defensive capabilities. But not Paul. He enjoyed nothing better than halting an attack by shepherding his opponent to the touchline, then chopping him down with a full-blooded tackle. Before long, it was acknowledged by many that he was the finest full-back of the modern era. Opponents always knew they were in for a tough afternoon when they came up against Paul in full flight.

The signings of Maurice Richards, Chris Hesketh, Mike Coulman and Keith Fielding had produced a brand of free-flowing rugby not seen at The Willows since the heady days of the Thirties when the side was led by Welsh-born legend Gus Risman. Salford were a formidable side rapidly becoming unaccustomed to defeat. Under the dynamic leadership of Brian Snape, they had been transformed into a glamour club, full of stars. This provided the perfect platform for Paul's skills as an attacking full-back to flourish. It also gave him the chance to etch his name in the record books by beating Tyrer's feat of scoring 21 tries in a season.

Paul did not so much break Tyrer's record. He smashed it to pieces when he landed 33 touchdowns in the 1972-73 season. He bagged 31 tries for Salford, one for Cumberland in their 26-16 defeat of Lancashire at Warrington, and one for Great Britain in their 53-19 World Cup victory over New Zealand in France. Paul began his prolific season in spectacular style when he scored a hat-trick for Salford in their 32-17 victory against his home-town team of Whitehaven. With barely half the season over, he clinched the record on December 13 1972 when he scored his 22nd try in a 14-12 win at Oldham. His further 11 tries included a second hat-trick of the season in a 30-4 win over Bradford Northern. Paul's achievement placed the try-scoring record for a full-back beyond the reach of any other player, and still stands more than a quarter of a century later.

But Paul was not the only Salford player to make it into the record books that season. The unique skills of team-mate David Watkins earned the former Welsh Rugby Union international an awesome reputation. His turn of speed and instinct for a gap saw him develop into one of Rugby League's most exciting players. Watkins, a stocky Welsh fly-half, made 21 appearances for his country, having graduated through Cwmcelyn youth team and Newport. Despite coming from the Union-mad Valleys, he went on to become a household name in the 13-man code. He joined Salford two seasons before Paul and repaid his £16,000 world record fee many times over.

The Salford captain's 100 goals in 18 matches in 1972-73 was a record at the time. By September 1973 he had passed the 100 points total for a season and was well on the way towards his record 471 points the previous season. In April he passed the 200 mark with four goals in a 17-7 victory over Widnes at The Willows. Only Ganley and Watkins's fellow Welshman Kel Coslett had ever scored a double century of goals.

Watkins was also closing in on Ganley's world record of 219 goals in a season, which had stood since 1958.

Going into the final league match of the season, Watkins was three behind. Salford were playing host to Wigan and went on to win 15-3 with the deadly boot of Watkins kicking three goals to equal the record.

With Salford in Championship play-off action, Watkins clinched the record with two goals in the first round against Rochdale.

A MAN FOR ALL SEASONS

AFTER Paul's magnificent record-breaking season of 1972-73 and his splendid World Cup campaign, he was an automatic choice in the Great Britain team for the visit of Australia the following season. The three-match Test series started at Wembley on November 3, 1973. They were games of huge importance. Not only was there national pride and personal glory at stake, but also places in the British Lions team for the tour of Australia and New Zealand at the end of the season.

International reputations were built or destroyed in Test matches against the Aussies. The competition for places was fierce. But Paul's inclusion in the team was seriously jeopardised by a late injury scare, which almost forced him to pull out of the game. Less than two weeks before the first Test, he broke his right thumb in three places in a clash with St Helens winger Roy Mathias. In typical style, Paul had played on, although he was in extreme pain after the game.

The following night he was supposed to be in action for Cumberland at Whitehaven's Recreation Ground, a game he was determined not to miss. Paul was captain of Cumberland, a responsibility he took with pride, and all his family and friends from his home town would be out in force to cheer him on and see him pick up his 21st county cap. Ron Morgan, the Cumberland team manager, faced an anxious wait to hear if his captain would make it. Paul was determined not to let him down.

With his right hand heavily strapped, Paul was part of a county team humbled 28-2 by the Australians, although his own contribution to a disappointing game lasted only until early into the second half. He faced more trauma after he popped a rib cartilage and had to be taken to Whitehaven's West Cumberland Hospital.

The first Test match was only ten days away and Paul was desperate not to miss it. With just three days to go before the game, to be beamed live on TV from Wembley, coach Jim Challinor called the British players to their training headquarters at Crystal Palace. Paul was a notable absentee. He decided to keep his injury worries to himself, and told Challinor he had a minor dose of the flu. His ploy worked and the extra 24 hours rest proved to be just what he needed.

The match was a hard-fought, exciting contest. Less than 10,000 fans were there to watch Britain's emphatic 21-12 victory but millions around the world tuned into the game on TV. Great Britain took the lead in the fourth minute and never surrendered it, holding a 12-point advantage after 50 minutes until Australia fought their way back to within two points in a tense second half. The visitors scored ten points in the space of four minutes to leave the game finely balanced. Phil Lowe, Terry Clawson and debutant David Topliss turned in impressive performances for Britain, who displayed the more cohesive team work. But it was not until the 72nd minute that they were assured of victory when Topliss created an opening for Lowe to race 30 yards for the match-winning try. Clawson kicked the conversion.

★ ★ ★

Historically, Headingley offered Great Britain a big advantage over the Australians. The Tourists had a poor record of nine Test defeats from nine visits to Leeds, and the scene seemed set for another British victory. However, Australia had three years earlier recorded a memorable World Cup victory at Headingley. Eight members of the 1973 Australian team were part of that triumph, which owed more to brutal tackling than skilful play.

In front of a crowd of 16,674, the Kangaroos put their Test match hoodoo behind them and proved worthy of their 14-6 win. They had learned their lessons from the previous encounter, while apart from Nash and Charlton, Britain were shadows of the team which had won so convincingly at Wembley. The visitors had done their homework and singled out players who posed the biggest threat. Britain's reliance on Lowe had been noted and he was met by droves of tacklers, while Bobby Fulton was an inspiration at stand-off for Australia. Captain Bob McCarthy ruled the forward exchanges until being forced to leave the pitch with an injury.

A dislocated shoulder, suffered while being tackled by Paul, meant the Aussie skipper was to be a key absentee in the deciding clash between the two teams at Warrington on December 1. The frost, which had cast a white blanket over the whole of the North West of England, left the third Test in serious danger of being called off.

★ ★ ★

Nearly 20 tons of straw had been laid to try to protect the pitch but the Great Britain team, which had assembled at a Cheshire hotel the day before the game, were almost certain it would not go ahead. Their doubts increased the night before as they left a cinema. The players walked gingerly along the slippery pavements back to their cars to find windscreens thick with ice. Yet, to the surprise of everyone, the game went ahead. The Arctic freeze had left the surface rock-hard and the tractor tyres had left deep, jagged ruts, which meant conditions were far from ideal for a free, flowing brand of rugby.

The Australians, playing in rubber studs, approached the game as if they were playing on their hard, sun-baked grounds back home and won the decider 15-5. They had won the Ashes for a third time in a row on English soil. Australia got off to an exciting start when Bobby Fulton, playing in the town of his birth, intercepted Clawson's short pass to Eckersley, and streaked away unchallenged to score in the corner.

There was little respite for Britain, who were forced to sustain relentless pressure from the Kangaroos. Shortly after the break, Britain's hopes were temporarily lifted when Roger Millward scored a well-worked try. But it succeeded only in galvanising the visitors into action. Britain had a scrum advantage of 16-8 and a penalty count of 7-4 in their favour but were still no match for the Aussies. They could provide little reply to man-of-the-series Artie Beetson and his band of fearless warriors.

LIONS GO INTO THE DEN

SELECTION for a British Lions Tour of Australasia is the greatest honour that can be bestowed on a Rugby League player. Many talented players have never been picked for a Tour, which comes round only once every four years. The newspapermen were predicting Paul would be the automatic choice for the full-back position for the 1974 Tour of Australia and New Zealand. But past experience had taught Paul never to take anything for granted. The huge disappointment of missing out on both the 1966 and 1970 tours still lingered at the back of his mind and, anyway, it wasn't in his nature to be cocky or over-confident. The three month-long tour began in May, but he had put all thoughts of it to one side to concentrate his efforts on helping Salford lift the Division One championship.

Paul and Lillian had also been preoccupied with building their new dream home back in Cumbria. Eight months earlier they had bought a plot of land in the picturesque village of St Bees on the coast, and Paul had set about building a beautiful bungalow. In the evenings and at weekends he would drive north from Salford, until "Charlo's" in Sea Mill Lane was finally ready for Lillian, Gary and Melanie to move in. Paul was determined to have it finished by May in case he was called up for the Tour, so that Lillian would be able to move in while he was overseas.

When he wasn't terrorising opposing defences, Paul was working as a carpenter helping to build a small housing estate not far from the family's current home in Kildare Road, between Walkden and Swinton. He may have been a sports star, waiting to hear if he had been picked to play for the British Lions, but he still had a living to make. As he wiped his forehead, damp with sweat from his tiring labour, he could see Lillian walking towards the building site. A secretary at Rugby League headquarters had just phoned her with the news that Paul was in the squad.

That evening champagne corks were popping in the Charlton household as Paul and Lillian toasted his success. It was going to mean three months apart but they had a strong marriage and they knew it would survive. Unlike many women of her generation, Lillian had learned to be self-sufficient and independent. Her husband's dedication to Rugby League could not have taught her to be anything different. But she wouldn't have had him any other way. Even more important than a Rugby League player's choice of club was his choice of wife. A woman not prepared to tolerate frequent long absences and her husband's devotion to duty would be destined for an unhappy marriage. Lillian was hugely supportive of Paul's career. She knew this was an opportunity he couldn't miss.

★ ★ ★

The squad assembled at Headingley for a roll call. Paul was joined by five Salford team-mates, Chris Hesketh, who was to captain the squad, Colin Dixon, Kenny Gill, Maurice Richards and David Watkins. They were kitted out with smart blazers, slacks, ties and shirts for formal occasions, plus training kits and tracksuits. The players were also weighed and measured and given a full medical check-up. The man in charge of the party was former England player Reggie Parker, a Challenge Cup winner with Barrow, the club he had joined as a professional in 1945. He was transferred to Wakefield Trinity in 1958, before joining Blackpool a few months later.

Parker, 46, ran a hotel with his wife Shirley in Grange-over-Sands in South Lakeland. Even though it would mean him abandoning the business at the peak of the tourist season, Shirley had encouraged her husband to put himself forward for the role of Tour manager. It was a plum job and it would be the experience of a lifetime for him.

Parker's assistant was Jim Challinor who started his career with Warrington in 1951. He then joined Barrow in 1963 as player-coach and became St Helens coach in 1970, leading them to the League Championship the following year and the Challenge Cup in 1972. Challinor, a quiet man, who was well liked by the players, had played for Great Britain in eight Tests and had been coach since 1971.

No one was surprised at the choice of Chris Hesketh as Tour captain. The 29-year-old paint salesman commanded the respect of his fellow internationals because of his experience and ability. Tough as a nut but intelligent and thoughtful, he was the right character for the demanding task of skipper. As a youngster, Hesketh had been handicapped after contracting polio. He was advised to play rugby to help him overcome the disease. His successful fight against the crippling disease and rise to the top as a sportsman made him an inspiration to others.

Prolific try scorer John Atkinson was the most experienced international on the Tour. The Leeds star played in the 1968 World Cup and in all six Tests against Australia and New Zealand in 1970. One of his most important tries came in the final clash at Sydney Cricket

Ground, which helped clinch Britain's Ashes triumph.

Australian fans would need no introduction to Roger Millward, who helped secure the Ashes trophy in 1970 with some spectacular performances. Roger The Dodger, as he was known, scored the winning try in the high-scoring Third Test at Sydney when it looked as if Britain would be robbed. After displacing Alan Hardisty at number six, Millward went on to claim 100 points by the end of the Tour. The Hull KR star was only 5ft 4in and weighed barely 10st, but he was blessed with a lightning-quick turn of pace which could destroy any defence.

Steve Nash flew out on the Tour with a deserved reputation as the world's top scrum-half. A brilliant tackler, his skill and tenacity helped make Featherstone Rovers one of the most feared sides in England.

Terry Clawson, from the Yorkshire heartland of Rugby League, was finding the going tough at the other side of the Pennines in Oldham. However, Great Britain selectors had wisely ignored criticism of the 15-stone prop, whose brilliant goal-kicking was an important part of the 1972 World Cup winning side.

Meanwhile, on the other side of the world, a new chapter was being added to the career of legendary Australian captain Graeme Langlands, that of coach of his country. The 32-year-old superstar first represented Australia in 1963 and had built up a formidable reputation. His gentle personality off the field never brought a flicker of compromise to his physical commitment on it. He suffered from that incurable condition so prevalent in top sportsmen – the refusal to accept defeat. John Sattler, an old colleague of Langlands, once said: "Graeme is a defeat hater".

Langlands's attitude epitomised the Australian spirit, which was to create the supremacy of the green and gold.

Meanwhile, the pain of parting was worse than Paul had imagined it would be as he hugged Lillian and his two children, knowing it would be the middle of August before he would see them again. The longest they had been apart was the two weeks of the World Cup in France in 1972, and Paul wondered how he would cope without his family for nearly three months, knowing they were at the other side of the world. Manchester Airport was packed with sun-seekers heading out for their annual holidays as the Great Britain squad said their farewells to their families. Paul boarded the plane for the adventure of a lifetime with a heavy heart. Some of his team-mates were in tears as the Quantas Airlines plane bound for Darwin, 12,000 miles away, took to the skies.

★ ★ ★

Paul's spirits soared. The telegram to the Oceanic Hotel in Coogee, New South Wales, was short and to the point but it gave him more motivation than any pre-match team talk.

It read simply: "Good luck, darling. Love you. Lily, Gary and Melanie".

It was just what he needed as Great Britain began their build-up to the first Test with a series of Tour matches.

They began their 28-match tour of the southern hemisphere with a convincing 41-2 victory over Darwin. Their perfect build-up to the first Test continued with further impressive wins over North Queensland, Central Queensland, Wide Bay, Ipswich and Queensland.

First Test, Lang Park, Brisbane
Australia 12 Great Britain 6

THE first Test failed to live up to the proud tradition and excitement of Anglo-Australian clashes. The tourists were punished for missed chances and silly mistakes in a lacklustre game in front of a crowd of 30,280, which included Australian Prime Minister Gough Whitlam.

Britain's only consolation was that Australia had shown they were not invincible. In fact, they looked quite ordinary. But by the time Britain had realised the limitations of their opponents, it was too late.

Perhaps ominously, Australia's victory was achieved without them being pushed to full stretch. The Kangaroos were always in front, even though they could score only a solitary try, while Britain hardly threatened to cross the line. For the Lions only Steve Nash and Roger Millward shone in defence.

British prop Terry Clawson summed up the British feelings afterwards when he admitted: "We were too soft with them.

"We should have made it hard for them as we did in the World Cup in 1972. This was not like a Test match at all".

Second Test, Sydney Cricket Ground, Sydney
Australia 11 Great Britain 16

The victory over Australia in the second Test would go down in history as one of the greatest displays of determination and spirit by a British Lions team.

Injuries had robbed them of many key players and they went into the game with only 13 fit players and several others on the pitch thanks only to pain-killing injections. All week Paul had been nursing a hamstring injury he had suffered in their 26-22 win over Illawarra, but, as ever, the gritty Cumbrian was determined not to miss the game. Les Dyl, Dave Eckersley and Roger Millward were all forced to play out of position and, in John Gray, they fielded a third choice hooker who, only a year, earlier had been playing Rugby Union.

Mike Stephenson, a former Great Britain player, was living Down Under playing for Penrith. He was approached about linking up with the squad, only for his club to block the move.

Before the game, Tour manager Parker had warned guests in one of his after-dinner speeches that an Englishman is at his most dangerous when everyone thinks he is down and out. Patched up and makeshift were just two of the descriptions of Parker's injury-ridden side, whose wonderful victory against all the odds would rank alongside the famous Rorke's Drift Test of 1914 and the Battle of Brisbane epic of 1958.

Despite the pre-match set-backs, Britain played with the confidence of a team at full strength and captured the hearts of the massive 48,006 crowd. Three stylish tries swept them into a 16-3 lead and the Lions never looked back.

Skipper Chris Hesketh could not hide his delight afterwards as he hailed his battling troops.

"I have never been so proud in my life", he said.

"We got up off the floor and came back from the dead. It was a brave performance that showed guts and character. Everyone gave everything they had."

Third Test, Sydney Cricket Ground, Sydney
Australia 22 Great Britain 18

Australia retained the Ashes. Fittingly, their victory was thanks to their captain Langlands, who brought down the curtain on his fabulous international career. Langlands became the first player to record 100 points in Test matches between the two nations. The match belonged to the veteran full-back right from the kick-off with a performance which must rank among his best in a green and gold shirt. He landed five goals and scored a try.

Even some spectacular goal-kicking by John Gray, who turned out to be one of the finds of the Tour, could not save Britain. Gray landed six goals from six attempts and won the scrums, but the Lions saw their 16-10 interval lead slowly reduced after a great comeback by the Kangaroos.

Britain were disappointing in the second half when too many tackles were missed. Bobby Fulton, Ron Coote and Langlands carved huge holes in their defence. There were also quiet mutterings about the partiality of the refereeing during the Tour. But coach Challinor said: "We will not use the referee as an excuse. We should have capitalised on our first half lead but we were not allowed to".

THE LIONS ROAR AT LAST

PAUL woke with a sudden jolt and sat upright in bed, quickly trying to gather his senses. He could hear shrieks of laughter and shouting coming from the corridor outside his hotel room.

"What on earth is that racket?" he asked his room-mate Chris Hesketh, who was also rousing from his slumber.

It had been a tiring journey from Australia to Auckland for the New Zealand leg of the tour. The pair had gone to bed early so they would be fresh for the next day's training. The clock on the cabinet next to Paul's bed said 1am. The two Great Britain players made their way to the door and froze in disbelief at the sight which greeted them.

Huge prop forward Jim Mills was hurtling down the corridor towards them, pushing a laundry trolley. Inside the trolley was burly second rower Colin Dixon, his arms and legs dangling over the side. Dixon's face was only just visible beneath a maid's frilly hat. Projecting from his mouth was a baby's dummy. The whole place was in uproar with team-mates following along behind in hysterical laughter. Hotel guests, who had also come dashing out of their rooms to see what the commotion was, stared in horror and tut-tutted, while others could barely contain their mirth. There was a disco downstairs at Auckland's Great Northern Hotel and most of the Great Britain players had gone to unwind after the long journey.

Suddenly, there were more footsteps in hot pursuit of the jokers and two huge, mean-looking Maori bouncers appeared around the corner. They took one look at the sight before them and the size of the men they had intended to apprehend and slinked quietly back to the nightclub.

It had been a gruelling tour of duty in Australia with 20 matches in a little over six weeks. The Great Britain players were naturally starting to feel tired. But they showed little sign of weakening as they faced up to another tough programme of three Test matches against New Zealand, plus a further five games against leading provincial sides.

No sooner had the dust settled on the defeat against Australia than preparations began for the New Zealand Test series. They were going into the series against the Kiwis as a better equipped and better prepared side than their opponents. In contrast to the battle-hardened Brits, New Zealand's build-up had been confined to just two low-key warm-up games.

There were also stars beginning to emerge in the British side after the Australian tour. Tours always seem to unearth gems and Britain's jewel-in-the-crown had turned out to be John Gray, originally included in the squad as a utility player – a forward who could switch to second or front row, but who was more at home as a hooker. There had been only a slight hint that the player with the flowing locks, who had played classical trumpet at big English concert halls, might win a Test place. As it turned out, he captured the imagination of the Australian crowds and earned the respect of the most experienced internationals. The man with the task of coping with Gray in the New Zealand series was Auckland hooker Bill Burgoyne who had toured with the Kiwis three times since 1970.

The home nation were strong in the backs, especially Ken Stirling and Dennis Williams, both of whom had played against Britain in 1971 when New Zealand were 2-1 winners. The matching of Stirling against scrum-half Steve Nash promised to be exciting. The battle on the wing was also a mouth-watering thought. The Canterbury pair of Mockey Brereton and exciting teenage prospect Eddie Kerrigan were up against Welsh wizards John Bevan and Maurice Richards.

Paul went into the series with his reputation as a full-back enhanced thanks to his running prowess and superb tackling which had saved his side many times in Australia. His New Zealand counterpart was the enterprising Auckland footballer Warren Collicoat who excelled in attack, especially from broken play.

Britain opened their account in New Zealand with a convincing 37-17 victory over North Island Country.

First Test
Carlaw Park, Auckland
New Zealand 13 Great Britain 8

Great Britain were never given a chance to get into their stride with the Kiwis adapting to the heavy going much better than the tourists.

New Zealand forwards John Greengrass, Doug Gailey, Tony Coll and Wayne Robertson were the home nation's key men. The quartet covered virtually every blade of grass and any chance Britain had of striking back was destroyed by some dubious refereeing decisions.

Referee John Percival penalised them 16 times, making it impossible to sustain any kind of attack. Team manager Parker called for him to be banned from officiating at any other tour games. It was also a game littered with controversy which later caused the New Zealand Rugby League authorities to launch an inquiry.

Very few Test matches were played without some sort of a brawl. This time it erupted in the 13th minute, while shortly afterwards later

Britain's Jimmy Thompson was knocked cold in a tackle by Doug Gailey. He was later forced to leave the field.

There was another moment of controversy soon afterwards when Paul, after fielding a high kick, lost the ball over the line when tackled by Greengrass, allowing Stirling to score. It prompted furious protests by the British that Greengrass had been offside at the kick and had also knocked on by forcing the ball from Charlton's grasp.

There was further woe for the Lions with another highly controversial refereeing decision. Greengrass was again at the centre of the drama. Colin Dixon was sent off in the 59th minute for an alleged high tackle on the second rower but it was a case of mistaken identity. Dixon, the only black player on the tour, was confused with a mud-soaked team-mate, whose identity was concealed by the conditions.

Second Test
Christchurch
New Zealand 8 Great Britain 17

British skipper Hesketh led by example with one of the best displays of the Tour to help level the series. Hesketh switched from centre to stand-off and turned in a match-winning performance. But the Lions left it until almost the last breath of the game before they could be sure of victory.

They began slowly but, once they found their feet, were more impressive than New Zealand, who seemed to have lost the ball-handling skills which played such a vital role in their first Test victory.

For Paul, however, the second Test ended prematurely and in disappointment after he was forced to limp off with a hamstring injury, which had dogged him throughout the New Zealand tour.

In-form hooker John Gray kept the Kiwis on their toes with his long clearances pushing them back into their own half. His four goals from acute angles gave the home nation an insight into the form which had caused Australia so many problems.

The game was deep into injury time when Steve Norton broke clear and Hesketh picked up a loose ball to side-step past the home defence and add to the two tries scored by Les Dyl and David Redfearn.

Third Test
Carlaw Park, Auckland
New Zealand 0 Great Britain 20

Thousands of miles of travelling eventually ended with a Great Britain triumph. Skipper Hesketh and his team returned home with a Test victory to savour.

The Lions built up a comfortable 8-0 lead early in the game and after that they were coasting to victory. Almost to a man, the British side had an air of supreme confidence about them as if defeat was never an option. It was perhaps the most complete team performance of the New Zealand tour. Their cause was helped by a disciplined display which gave referee John Percival no excuse to penalise them for technical offences.

There were early signs that the tie might just go Britain's way when Colin Dixon, John Gray and John Bevan all found gaps. The speed of Hesketh was a constant danger to New Zealand, while Gray's goal-kicking was again spot on.

The Kiwis battled on in vain and managed to keep the game flowing but Britain could not be denied an emphatic victory.

The Great Britain squad left New Zealand convinced of two things, firstly neutral referees were a must for future Test matches Down Under and, secondly, the decision to increase the number of tackles from four to six had been a wise move.

After three years playing six tackles, the Tourists found the New Zealand game, where the four-tackle rule was still used, too much like kick and rush. It had provided much-needed ammunition for those calling for more uniformity in the game.

As well as the victory in New Zealand, Britain could claim another success. They brought back with them from the tour record profits of £93,282.

★ ★ ★

The journey home seemed to take forever for the squad, who were now weary after a punishing three months on the road. They had travelled thousands of miles and were homesick for their families, which made the troubled journey home all the worse. The war in Cyprus was causing disruption in the Middle East and it resulted in their plane being stranded on the tarmac at Beirut.

They eventually arrived at Heathrow, ready to catch a British Airways flight to Manchester, where their wives and children would be waiting for them.

But the ground steward had bad news for them. They would have to wait a further three hours and travel on a later flight at 10pm. The players were up in arms and surrounded the hapless steward in protest.

"You can see how big these lads are and I'm not asking them to move", said tour manager Reggie Parker.

"I'm sure we'll be able to sort something out if you can just give me a few minutes", replied the steward.

At 7pm Parker and his players were boarding the plane to Manchester, home to their loved ones – and the start of the new season.

HOME SWEET HOME

"CHARLTON – you're a load of rubbish!" shouted an irate Keighley supporter as Paul and his Salford team-mates trudged dejectedly off the Lawkholme Lane pitch. It was only the first game of the season but Salford looked mere shadows of the side which had won the championship in such wonderful style the previous season.

The men from The Willows had provided the backbone of the British Lions squad and the exhausting Tour Down Under had taken its toll. Salford's six internationals had flown home only a week before the season started. Understandably they looked jaded after such a demanding summer. Like Paul, some were still carrying the knocks and strains they had picked up on the Tour. Keighley's supporters were only too eager to let Paul know he was not yet back to his best.

A return to form ensured Paul remained a first team regular at Salford but he gradually began to realise the 1974-75 season might well be his last with the club. He was fast approaching 33 and he knew he did not have a long-term future at The Willows. Stories had been circulating in the papers that Andy Irvine, the Heriots and Scotland RU full-back, was being lined up as his successor. Although he had achieved some of the greatest honours in the game with a League Championship and Lancashire Cup winners' medals and had also shone on an international stage, Paul accepted he had no divine right to a first team place.

If he was to leave Salford, his destination was almost certainly his old club Workington Town. At the insistence of Workington supremo Tom Mitchell, when he was sold to Salford, there was a clause in his contract that the Cumbrian club would have first refusal if he ever became available. Unknown to Paul, a question mark was hanging over the future of Town coach Ike Southward. Mitchell had Paul in mind as his replacement. It made perfect sense for Paul to consider a return to his roots. He and his family had been living in St Bees for several months. He had been commuting to Salford three times a week for training and games. The travelling was beginning to become a burden.

At the end of the season, the transfer back to Derwent Park was completed for a fee of £500. Paul had a heavy heart at leaving Salford, but the opportunity to move into coaching presented him with a fresh challenge.

During his time at The Willows he had achieved his Level Three coaching badge at Lilleshall. Ron Morgan, the Cumberland team manager and former Whitehaven coach, was the North West region's Rugby League coach. Morgan ran clinics to teach others how to coach youngsters, before they returned to their home area to spread the gospel.

Paul and his former Workington team-mate Phil Kitchin were two of Morgan's protégés and they were leading lights in forming the enviable youth set-up in West Cumbria. Rugby League hot-beds such as Cleator Moor, Wath Brow and Hensingham, which had previously not catered for youngsters, formed children's teams, playing in a new youth league. The intention was to groom kids for the future so they could then feed into the senior teams. Paul, though, had no experience of coaching professionals. He was only too aware that just because you were a good player, it didn't necessarily follow that you would become a successful coach. Nevertheless, his return to Derwent Park was greeted with an air of expectation by supporters and players.

Paul inherited a team which oozed the potential to be a force in the game once again. After narrowly missing out on promotion at the end of the 1974 season, they were left disappointed again the following season. They ended the 1974-75 season in fifth place in Division Two, but with their reputation enhanced. Workington had begun to show signs that they were on the upgrade and were only a couple of players short of being promotion contenders.

In the Challenge Cup, they had beaten Barrow in the first round but the draw for the second round had not been kind. They faced the longest possible journey to Hull KR and it ended in a 19-7 defeat. However, the scoreline had not done justice to a fighting performance by Town, who had looked the better side until stand-off John Dobie was carried off with a knee injury.

The Players No. 6 Trophy was also a disappointment. They went out in the first round after a 21-14 defeat at the hands of Oldham. Workington had better luck in the Lancashire Cup and enjoyed another impressive run. In the first round they defeated St Helens 13-11 at Knowsley Road and were rewarded with a home tie with Swinton. A 17-7 victory, thanks to four goals from the boot of Iain MacCorquodale and tries from Arnold "Boxer" Walker, Ian Wright and John Risman, took them into the semi-finals for the second season running.

Ironically, their fine run in the cup came to an end against Paul's side, Salford, who proved too strong on their home territory. Town bowed out 17-10 but had not been disgraced against one of the best sides in the country.

Unlike Salford, the squad Paul took over at Workington did not contain any big stars, earning huge amounts of money. But he could boast a band of tough Cumbrians, prepared to run through a brick wall for their club.

Britain's 1972 World Cup-winning party about to fly out to France. Back row: (L to R) Mick Naughton (referee), Clive Sullivan, David Redfearn, John Atkinson, John Holmes, Bill Fallowfield (RL secretary), Brian Lockwood, Wilf Spaven (manager), George Nicholls, Ron Simpson (RL Council), Unknown, Terry Clawson, Phil Lowe, David Jeanes, Colin Dixon, John Walshe, Jim Challinor, Dennis Wright (physio). Front row: Mike Stephenson, Steve Nash, Tony Karalius, David Topliss, Dennis O'Neil, Chris Hesketh, Paul Charlton, Bob Irving.

The Salford Six pictured at the famous Sydney Cricket Ground. Six players from The Willows were selected for Great Britain's 1974 Tour of Australia and New Zealand. Standing: Paul, Chris Hesketh, Colin Dixon, Maurice Richards. Kneeling: Ken Gill and David Watkins.

Rugby League News Souvenir

1974 GT. BRITAIN TOURING TEAM

The Great Britain squad which toured Australia and New Zealand in 1974. Back row (left to right): Jim Challinor (coach), Steve Norton, Les Dyl, George Nicholls, Terry Clawson, Chris Hesketh (Capt.), John Bates, John Bridges, John Atkinson, Dave Eckersley, Reggie Parker (manager). Middle: Paul Rose, Jim Thompson, Colin Dixon, Paul Charlton, John Bevan, Jim Mills, Dave Redfearn, Eric Chisnall, Dave Willicombe, Kevin Ashcroft. Front: Steve Nash, John Butler, Alan Bates, Roger Millward, Dave Watkins, Ken Gill, John Gray.

Australia's 1974 Test side. Back row (left to right): Warren Orr, Bob O'Reilly, Arthur Beetson, Ron Coote, Mick Cronin. Middle: Ray Higgs, Elwyn Walters, Paul Sait, David Waite, Geoff Richardson, John Lang. Front: Tom Raudonikis, Ralph Stafford (manager), Graeme Langlands (captain-coach), Alf Richards (trainer), Bobby Fulton.

Inspirational skipper Chris Hesketh leads out Great Britain in the First Test against Australia followed by Paul and Roger Millward.

Paul congratulates St Helens star Eric Chisnall after his try in Great Britain's 11-16 victory over Australia in the Second Test.

Paul and Great Britain colleague John Gray challenge for the ball. Gray turned out to be one of the finds of the Tour. In the Third Test he landed six goals from six attempts.

Well done dad! Children Gary and Melanie proudly hold Paul's treasured Great Britain shirt following his return home to St Bees, in Cumbria.

Lillian joins in the celebrations as the family show off Paul's Tour medals. Paul and his team-mates were away on Tour for three months and it was painful parting from their families at Manchester Airport.

Back where it all started. Paul rejoined Workington Town as player-coach in 1975. He led them to promotion to Division One in his first season in charge.

Gorley in his glory. Peter Gorley followed in brother Les's footsteps by joining Town and later won Great Britain honours.

Les Gorley, whose 16st frame caused havoc among Workington's opponents. A key member of the 1977 Lancashire Cup-winning side.

Eddie Bowman, a powerful second-rower whose physique was developed working as a fitter down Haig Pit. Expensive signing from Whitehaven in 1970.

Arnold "Boxer" Walker in his Great Britain shirt. As a schoolboy he would watch his idol Paul Charlton practise his goal-kicking on Kells playing field and retrieve the balls for him.

Ike Southward was one of Rugby League's all-time greats. Workington sold him to Oldham for a world record fee of £10,065 in 1959. He replaced Paul as coach in 1976.

Paul surrounded by young fans during a coaching session in Workington. Paul played a big part in developing Rugby League at grassroots level in West Cumbria.

A TEAM OF CUMBRIAN HEROES

WINE, women and song were Arnold "Boxer" Walker's main loves in life but behind the wayward image lay a unique talent. A self-confessed bad-boy, he enjoyed his reputation as a hard man on the pitch almost as much as he loved a post-match pint. There were times when Boxer exasperated Paul with his antics but there was a deep bond between them which was nurtured in their home town of Whitehaven.

The pair were like chalk and cheese – Boxer the fearless extrovert, Paul shy and withdrawn. Despite the differences, Boxer idolised Paul. As a schoolboy, he would spend his evenings at Kells playing field watching Paul practise his goal-kicking. Paul, who was then making a name for himself with Workington, would kick the ball between the posts and Boxer would run to retrieve it like a faithful terrier.

Boxer was 11 years younger than Paul. He was born in the same part of Whitehaven, the hamlet of Woodhouse. The similarities did not end there. Boxer also began his playing career with Kells amateur side, which his father Duncan, a miner at Haig Pit, helped run. It was while playing for Kells at the British Legion pitch in Maryport in front of a handful of spectators that Boxer was spotted by Workington chairman Mitchell. Mitchell was a frequent visitor to Kells games and was sufficiently impressed by the scrawny-looking teenager to make a note of his name.

By the time Boxer was 17, a host of top clubs, including Hull Kingston Rovers, Warrington, Barrow, Whitehaven and Leeds had joined the queue for his signature. He rebuffed Mitchell three times before finally, in a car park in Grasslot, Maryport, he scribbled his signature on the back of a cigarette packet in exchange for a £750 signing-on fee. After a short spell in the A team, he made his debut against Huyton in October 1971, scoring the winning try in the last five minutes.

Boxer stood only 5ft 6in and weighed little over 10st. But his tough, uncompromising style of play and willingness to take on men nearly twice his size belied his stature. A big toothless grin was his trademark. If he left the pitch without a busted nose or bleeding lip, he didn't feel as if he had done his job.

As a coach, Paul demanded discipline from his players. He was self-motivated and utterly dedicated, and he expected the same high standards from them. Players had to be at training by 6.30pm prompt. On match days he insisted on a dress code of shirt, tie, smart slacks and

Workington Town blazers. Sometimes he would shout so loudly on the training pitch that he would suddenly lose his voice. The players would be reduced to giggles at the barely-audible croaks coming from their coach, and Paul was always quick to see the funny side too.

Instilling more discipline into the side was partly responsible for Workington's success during his first season as coach, but Paul was realistic enough to know he was fighting a losing battle with Boxer, no matter how hard he tried to keep him under control. Boxer regarded brushes with authority as an occupational hazard.

In Paul's first season in charge, Workington were pressing for promotion and had an important game with Blackpool Borough looming. Although the club had a strict no-drinking policy the night before games, Boxer frequently flouted the rules. On the eve of the big match he went to his local pub for a couple of pints, where he bumped into an old friend. The man had a bottle of brandy with him and, hearing about Boxer's pre-match nerves, offered him a drink.

"Put that in your mouth and have a good swig," he told him.

Boxer went home legless.

Bleary-eyed and nursing a dreadful headache, he managed to catch the team bus in time for the trip to Lancashire. As always, the team was scheduled to stop at a steak bar near Kendal for a pre-match meal, but just the thought of tucking into gammon and a fried egg made Boxer feel even more queasy.

"Just stay on the bus and don't have anything to eat or you'll feel even worse," advised team-mate Eddie Bowman.

As the rest of the players trooped into the restaurant, Paul, suspecting something was amiss, went to the back of the coach to find out why Boxer wasn't his usual effervescent self. The answer was clearly written in the scrum-half's bloodshot eyes. Paul glowered at him. Boxer scurried off the coach and forced down his meal. Boxer knew he was going to have to do something special on the field that afternoon to avoid being carpeted so he hatched a plan to follow Paul and Eddie to make sure he was at the end of every pass. It worked a treat. Boxer returned home clutching yet another man-of-the-match award for his hat-trick of tries in Workington's 25-8 win.

Boxer possessed another talent. The ability to wind people up. Not only did he enjoy provoking 18st props on the field, he also liked nothing better than pulling the legs of his team-mates off the pitch. On the away trip to Doncaster, Paul, who boasted the ability to shepherd players towards the touchline before tackling them, misjudged a situation. A big prop managed to skirt past him and dived over the line at the corner flag. Even though it made no difference to Town's 44-8 winning margin, Paul took his mistakes to heart and was still cursing himself after the game.

Back on the bus Boxer decided to capitalise on his friend's rare lapse.

"Hey Charlo, you've lost about five yards on your pace," he goaded him.

The teasing continued as Boxer, Paul and Derek McMillan shared the car journey home from Workington.

Two days later the trio were travelling to training when Paul said: "Boxer you were right, I have lost a few yards".

Paul, who prided himself on his fitness, had been so distraught at allowing his opponent to score that he had taken the mickey-taking to heart. As soon as he had got home, while his players enjoyed their post-match drinks, he spent an hour sprint training on St Bees beach.

Boxer shook his head. "I divven't believe thou, Charlton", he said. "I'll nivver be as dedicated as you."

★ ★ ★

Another product of Kells amateur team was Eddie Bowman. A fitter at Haig Pit, Bowman had started his career in the backs but, after growing up in all directions, he switched to the second row. Jim Brough signed him for Whitehaven and began building his team around the powerful, big-hitting six-footer. Leigh tried to prise him away from the Recreation Ground for £10,000, but it was Tom Mitchell's persuasive powers which lured him to Workington in 1970. He joined them in exchange for three other players, including Dennis Martin, plus around £4,000.

Second-row forward Les Gorley was really two players in one, a battering ram with the subtlety of a stand-off. Opponents who felt the full weight of his 16st frame and the effects of his creative ability were in no doubt of that. A joiner from Great Broughton, near Cockermouth, he had joined Workington in 1970. Five years later he was joined by his younger brother Peter.

The younger Gorley was a late developer physically, but he had successfully overcome the burden of attempting to follow an older brother whose quality shone through at an earlier age.

Iain MacCorquodale was snapped up as a bargain buy from Salford in 1972 and he went on to become one of Town's most prolific points scorers. It had taken hours of persuasion by Mitchell to tempt MacCorquodale to join Workington. When Mitchell had approached him, he was met with the response: "I know who you are and if you think you are going to get me up there you are mistaken. No chance!"

But Mitchell was not a man to take no for an answer and soon he had captured the master goal-kicker. The Oldham teacher's huge appetite for goals was matched by his boundless enthusiasm for the game. They were two qualities which played a significant part in helping Workington gain promotion.

If Workington fans were expecting something special from Paul's return, they were not to be disappointed. The season ended in triumph with Town finishing third in the league to clinch promotion back to Division One. The success was a tribute to the team spirit which had been developed at Derwent Park.

The Workington team went through the whole 1975-76 season unbeaten away from home in the league. They slipped up four times at Derwent Park but promotion meant they were quickly forgiven by supporters.

On October 5 Paul had reached a personal milestone when he clocked up his 250th game for the club, while Les Gorley, Iain MacCorquodale and Alan Banks all completed 100 games. The success in his first season in charge had exceeded Paul's own expectations, but he still felt some uneasiness at combining playing with coaching. Coaching a team was a demanding enough role without having to worry about his own performances on the field.

No sooner had the dust settled on the season, than Paul was summoned to Salmon Hall, the country home of Tom Mitchell in Seaton, near Workington. Mitchell had suspected Paul had misgivings about the dual role and he wanted a chat with him about his future. The pair talked long into the evening and it was decided he would continue as club captain but relinquish his coaching duties for the coming season. Ike Southward would once again take up the reins.

TOWN'S CUP OF JOY

ONLY the sentimental were backing Workington Town to beat Wigan in the 1977 Lancashire Cup final at Warrington. The cool heads needed no convincing that Wigan's team of all-stars would lift the trophy for the 17th time, while Workington's 32-year wait would go on.

They had come so close to breaking their hoodoo when they reached the final against Widnes the previous year, just months after Southward had replaced Paul as coach. The result hung in the balance right up until the final hooter but Town ended up narrowly losing 16-11 after their nerves got the better of them.

Town's route to the 1977 final had seen them take the scalp of Swinton in the opening round, before they comfortably disposed of Blackpool Borough 30-8 to set up an away tie with Warrington in the semi-final. The match at Wilderspool ended 9-9, before Town won the replay 26-15 to reach a second successive final.

Rumours spread that Wigan second-rower Bill Ashurst had placed a £100 bet with the bookies on his side winning the cup. It was a bold wager, more than a week's pay to many people. Wigan were so confident of winning, their club had even arranged a celebration buffet for their officials and players at Central Park that evening. The news got back to the Workington players but it did nothing to dent their confidence. It merely fired them up more, not only to win, but to do it in style.

The atmosphere in the Workington dressing room was one of determi-nation as conditioner Andy Key gave the players a final soothing massage before they strapped themselves up. There was a quiet confidence among the players.

The team had stopped off for a light lunch at Charnock Richard service station on the M6 motorway. It was a chance to stretch their legs and relax. Boxer Walker and Eddie Bowman were selecting records on the juke box as the other players finished their lunch or chatted about the game over a cup of tea. As Boxer put the money into the slot, he turned to his friend and said: "You know something Eddie, we're going to beat them today".

Bowman looked him straight in the eye and replied: "I know we are".

Kick-off was looming ominously nearer as the bus inched its way through a traffic jam on the outskirts of Warrington. It did nothing to soothe the pre-match nerves. Eventually a police motorcyclist arrived to guide the bus to Wilderspool.

A sea of smiling faces shouting good luck messages greeted the players as they tried to make their way into the ground. The final had captured the hearts and imaginations of Town supporters, and an army of more than 5,000 fans had travelled from Cumbria. Back home, shops and houses were decked in blue and white for two weeks before the game. Those who had not joined the exodus, were waiting by their radios.

Wigan may have gone into the game with confidence flowing and their game plan fine-tuned, but they had bargained without the unquenchable Workington spirit. It was an afternoon when true Cumbrian grit shone through. The match was dramatic, tense and action-packed, and hinged on ferocious first-time tackling and strong running by Town's forwards.

The boot of Iain MacCorquodale sank Wigan's hopes in the first 20 minutes of the second half with three memorable penalty goals. The last of the three was a mammoth 50-yarder to put Workington into a 15-8 lead.

Powerful prop Eddie Bowman never touched the ball without doing something constructive with it. Boxer Walker's inspirational performance again deservedly won him the man-of-the-match award and maintained his record of dropping a goal in every round of the competition.

Town's pack boasted a mighty triumvirate at the back – Bill Pattinson and Les and Peter Gorley, while in the centres, John Risman was strong and intimidating and Ian Wright stylish and elusive.

The first of Town's two tries came in the 10th minute when Les Gorley broke away and released Ian Wright to touch down.

Wigan took the lead for the only time when centre Dave Willicombe cut inside and scored, with Jim Nulty kicking the conversion.

Town were soon back in front when Peter Gorley powered his way through for Ray Wilkins to score their second try of the afternoon.

It wasn't all plain sailing. Town had to withstand a strong fightback by Vince Karalius's side. Green Vigo, Wigan's ace try scorer, led his side's resistance but Town stood strong to keep them at bay and win 16-13.

As the full-time hooter sounded, chairman Mitchell raced on to the pitch, waving his famous blue crushed velvet fedora hat in the air, before planting it on the head of Peter Gorley and embracing his other conquering heroes. Town's battle-weary warriors raised their arms in delight, while others sank to their knees as if in prayer.

Paul had not been able to finish the game. He had limped off with

10 minutes to go, but the pain paled into insignificance as he led Town's heroes up the steps through the back-slapping and hair-ruffling. He wiped his muddy hands on his jersey, before lifting the cup aloft. It was one of the proudest moments of a career, and it assured him of a place in history as one of the all-time greats. A World Cup winner's medal, a Division One Championship medal, 19 appearances for Great Britain, one for England, Cumbrian honours and now a second Lancashire Cup medal. It had been some career.

After the game, he told reporters: "What a great feeling it is. When I stood up there and saw all the blue and white scarves, a lump came to my throat. They are the best supporters in the land".

Workington Town: Charlton, Collister, Risman, Wright, MacCorquodale, Wilkins, Walker, Watts, Banks, Bowman, L. Gorley, P. Gorley, Pattinson, Atkinson, Hartley.

★ ★ ★

The team celebrations continued long into the night as the players toasted their success at the 200 Club back at Derwent Park. The following week there was a civic reception at the town hall. The players had hardly been able to make it inside after being mobbed by jubilant supporters. Their route through the front entrance of the building was blocked by the cheering, scarf-waving crowd, so the players had to be diverted through the back door, where they were greeted by civic dignitaries.

Tom Mitchell had promised the players a sunshine break if they won the Lancashire Cup at the end of the season. He remained true to his word. The team piled onto the coach for the journey to Glasgow Airport, where they would catch a flight to Benidorm. Now the celebrations could really begin.

It was a new experience for most of the players. Apart from Paul and Eddie Bowman, who had both been on Great Britain tours, none of them had been abroad. Bowman walked up the aisle of the bus and told each of his team-mates not to forget their passports when they got off the coach. His warnings began to irritate the others and Boxer eventually told him to sit down and stop being "high and mighty".

The flight was delayed but the players consoled themselves with a few more drinks in the bar, chatting to other holiday-makers and signing autographs. After a two hour delay, they were called to the departure lounge by a stewardess. The party made their way along the corridor ready to board the plane when suddenly Bowman let out a shriek.

"You're not going to believe this, lads", he said, frantically searching his pockets.

"I've forgotten my passport."

It was no joke. The red-faced second-rower had left his travel documents on the coach, which was now on its way back to West Cumbria.

As coach, Ike Southward may have been used to conducting delicate negotiations but persuading the airline to allow his player onto the flight, was an achievement in itself.

After all the pre-flight drama, the players finally arrived at Benidorm's Hotel Calypso. Deano's Bar became the regular haunt. By night, they drank and danced into the early hours to the music from the film Saturday Night Fever. By day, they lazed by the pool. A trip to a barbecue at another resort 12 miles away was planned for the middle of the week. The Hotel Calypso had arranged a bus to transport guests to the barbecue, where there would be food, drink and entertainment from a local band. The evening went with a swing and the players returned to the hotel in good spirits, just in time to catch the late bar. But there was something troubling Boxer, who was casting an anxious eye around the room.

"Oh no, we've left Charlo behind!" he gasped.

An hour later Paul eventually arrived back at the hotel in a taxi, convinced he had been victim of a prank and heading straight in Boxer's direction.

The week was drawing to a close and the players had bought presents for their wives and children, but Bowman was growing increasingly anxious. His travel documents had still not arrived from the British Embassy. He had no alternative but to contact his wife Sandra and explain to her that he was going to have to stay behind for another couple of days until an emergency passport arrived. And that passport drama still had one act left to run.

The Town players had their suitcases packed ready to leave for the airport with their flight ready to depart in less than two hours. Boxer, who had decided to learn from Bowman's mistake, had left his passport in the hotel safe so on their way out of the hotel to went to reception to retrieve it. The other players looked at each other in wide-eyed disbelief as Boxer was informed that only the hotel manager had a key for the safe and he had gone home for the weekend.

As the team coach left for the airport, they were waved off by Boxer, Eddie and Derek McMillan, who had decided to extend his holiday anyway.

THE MENTOR

IT seemed the most unlikely of friendships. On the one hand was the millionaire eccentric intellectual and on the other a working class lad from a Whitehaven council estate. But as soon as Tom Mitchell and Paul Charlton met, there was an instant mutual appreciation.

They shared a common bond capable of uniting all classes and backgrounds – Rugby League. They also recognised in each other ambition and a single-minded determination to be successful. These were two traits Mitchell immediately spotted in Paul before he had even broken into the Workington first team.

Mitchell had taken a phone call from chairman Jim Graves one day, appealing to him to give the young Charlton his chance in the side to stop the youngster pestering the life out of him!

Mitchell likened Paul to Gus Risman, captain of Great Britain's 1946 Australian Tour, whom he rated as his greatest signing of all-time when he joined Town from Salford.

Their friendship was cemented during the team holiday in Benidorm after the Lancashire Cup win. The players had spent the week celebrating in the bars and clubs in the sunshine resort but it wasn't really Paul's scene. He enjoyed the occasional drink and was blessed with a good sense of humour but he was different to the other players. He wasn't an extrovert. He was quiet and reserved with a hint of natural shyness and modesty about his playing achievements. They were qualities which people inside and outside the game had come to respect and admire, especially Mitchell. While the other players would enjoy a few beers in the players' lounge after games, Paul would sip a lager shandy before saying his goodbyes and heading off home.

Mitchell had not flown out to Benidorm with the players. He had business to attend to in Vienna, so he later joined up with them for two nights. The players left for another night on the town. In a quiet corner of the hotel bar there remained Paul and Tom. It was early evening and Paul was drinking his usual coke, while Tom enjoyed a pint or two. Six hours later, long after the players had returned and gone to bed, the pair were still sitting putting the world of Rugby League to rights and discussing the future of the club.

"You know something Charlton," Mitchell told him, in his straight-talking, no-nonsense manner. "You've always been completely uncoachable. You've got your own skills and we just have to adapt our game to you because we always knew no coach in the world could change you."

With his huge bushy beard, distinctive hat and air of mystery, Mitchell was one of Rugby League's most colourful, flamboyant and controversial figures. He had the ability to shock, not only with his forthright manner and views, but also with his foppish appearance. He had supporters and players alike rubbing their eyes in disbelief when he arrived at a game at Widnes wearing a corduroy cap, dark sunglasses, trainers and an outrageous full-length fur coat.

On another occasion, while the players and coach Billy Ivison were having a post-match drink in the Warrington bar, he ordered Ivison to go and collect the hat he had earlier left on the table in the boardroom. The players, led by Phil Kitchin, were incensed, and appealed to Ivison not to bow to Mitchell's request. Unfortunately for Ivison, following his players' advice proved an unwise move. Mitchell immediately sacked him, although he reinstated his coach once the storm in a hat-rack had blown over a week later.

Behind Mitchell's flamboyant image was one of the most influential figures in Rugby League. His association with Workington was born out of a love of sport. The farmer's son from West Cumbria played both football and rugby union at Workington Grammar School.

The youngest of three children, his father, Tom senior, had wanted him to take over the running of his two farms but his mother Mary was determined her son would receive a top-level education. Mitchell had grown up in farming. He kept 10 hens in his father's orchard. When they laid, he received pocket money for selling the eggs. His father would also pay him the princely sum of 3p for every 100 yards of weeding he did in the potato and turnip plots.

Mary was so determined her son would receive a good education that she earned extra money by repairing the farm labourers' clothes by hand. After leaving the grammar school, Mitchell attended Newton Rigg College in Penrith, and won a scholarship to King's College, now Newcastle University. There he studied organic chemistry and bacteriology, before going to Leeds to study for a National Diploma in Agriculture. He completed a post-graduate course at Cambridge and began working life as a district officer on the war agriculture executive committee, covering the 38 parishes of West Cumberland. But Mitchell was destined to become a higher flyer than this. He continued to work in the civil service on top secret work for the Government all over the world.

Just after World War Two the directors of Workington Reds football club decided to form a Rugby League club. Three months later they invited Mitchell to join the board. He helped form a three-man team-building committee to set up Workington Town, but while the other two directors devoted their efforts to the soccer club, Mitchell headed a committee working closely alongside chairman Jim Graves.

Mitchell's rise to prominence in the game led to him being appointed team manager of the 1958 Great Britain side which toured Australia and took the Ashes with a 2-1 series win. There were six Town men in the party, Mitchell, coach Jim Brough and players Ike Southward, Harry Archer, Brian Edgar and Bill Wookey.

One down in the Test series after an opening 25-8 defeat with Mitchell's reputation as manager called into question, Britain were down to just eight fit players for the second game. This was the scene of the celebrated Battle of Brisbane, which was to go down in history as one of the most heroic displays in sport.

The players arrived for the game mentally and physically exhausted after the exertions of the first clash, but their unbreakable spirit and courage owed everything to the immense pride of wearing an international shirt.

After 17 minutes Britain were down to 12 men when stand off David Bolton went off with a broken collar bone. The injury toll continued to mount. Full-back Eric Fraser burst a blood vessel and could hardly use his arm, while centre Jim Challinor had to battle on with a badly bruised shoulder.

Vince Karalius, the "Wild Bull of Pampas", couldn't move at half-time because of a temporary paralysis of the spine, but the most incredible display of bravery came from captain Alan Prescott, who played on despite breaking his arm after only five minutes.

Britain faced the might of the tough Australian forwards with a four-man pack. After the game eight players had to go to hospital for treatment. Britain led throughout, and just as they began to wonder if they could hold out against all the odds, Southward scored two tries between the posts. Amazingly, Britain won 25-18 and went on to win the Ashes.

The Battle of Brisbane was also a personal triumph for Mitchell. It ranks as one of the most satisfying moments of his Rugby League career. He has no doubt which ranks as the saddest: that was the day Paul Charlton was sold to Salford.

THE SANDS OF TIME

WORKINGTON'S bitter-sweet love affair with the Lancashire Cup continued when they reached their third successive final in October 1978. They met Widnes, the team which had broken their hearts in the final two years earlier, at Central Park. But their hopes of repeating the previous season's famous victory over Wigan were shattered in a disastrous end to the game.

From the second minute, when Welsh centre Ray Wilkins scored a try, until 10 minutes before the end, Town looked certain winners as they took a commanding 13-5 lead. Then, amid chants of "easy, easy" from Town's supporters, it all went horribly wrong. Widnes grabbed two converted tries in the space of three minutes.

The match was not without controversy with Paul right at the centre of it. Town left Central Park convinced that the only reason Stuart Wright had been able to score the equalising try seven minutes from time was that Paul had been obstructed by Mal Aspey, whose shirt pulling forestalled the tackle.

After narrowly avoiding relegation in their previous two seasons, the league picture looked slightly brighter for Workington in the 1978-79 season. They finished in ninth position, narrowly missing out on a place in the Premiership play-offs.

Like all exponents of a dangerous art, Rugby League players know the hazards which can befall them. But nothing could have prepared Workington Town for the shock of the horrific injury suffered by popular stand-off John Burke. The day after his 21st birthday, Burke was left paralysed for life after he suffered a double neck fracture in a match against Leeds at Derwent Park.

The gruesome injury devastated the team and provided a chilling reminder of the perils players faced every time they stepped onto the pitch.

The injury happened in the first half of the game when his neck snapped in a tackle after he had taken a pass at an awkward angle. It had seemed an innocuous challenge, but as Burke lay motionless on the ground, it became apparent something much more serious had happened. Town physio John Short knew there was something dangerously wrong. Burke, whose £11,000 transfer fee from Wigan mid-way through the previous season was the third highest ever paid by the club, was carefully taken to West Cumberland Hospital.

The following day he was taken on a tortuous ambulance journey to the spinal injuries unit 70 miles away in Hexham, where his wife Jackie was told there was only a slim chance of her husband ever walking again. Burke, who had been one of the fittest athletes in the team, was left with the prospect of spending the rest of his life in a wheelchair.

A trust fund was set up to raise £50,000 to buy a specially-adapted bungalow for the popular former Wigan stand-off and his family.

The accident was to overshadow the whole season.

Paul reached another milestone in his career when on September 17, 1978, he clocked up his 350th game for the club. It was a remarkable achievement, but it was surpassed 18 months later when he firmly carved his name in the history of the club. The home defeat against York on January 6, 1980 saw him make his 398th appearance, a record for a Town player, overtaking Sol Roper's 397 appearances.

Paul was now 39. He may still have been fitter than many men half his age thanks to his devotion to the game, but not even Paul could tackle the sands of time. The following season he could manage only three appearances after being beset by injury problems, inevitable for a player who had played more than 700 first class games. He had undergone a cartilage operation during the close season, and since then had been plagued with achilles tendon and neck trouble. It opened the way for talented newcomer Graham Hogg to stake a claim as his successor in the number one shirt.

The personal turmoil for Paul was mirrored in that of the club as a whole with big changes sweeping through Derwent Park. The team, which had been on the threshold of success during the late Seventies, gradually began to break up.

Boxer Walker was transferred to arch-rivals Whitehaven, John Risman, Harry Beverley and Iain MacCorquodale all joined new club Fulham, Alan Banks signed for Blackpool Borough and Ian Wright and Ray Wilkins both decided to call it a day.

Keith Irving, who had occupied the coach's post for less than six months, decided to quit in November 1980. The team had just one win from 12 league and cup matches. The long-serving Ike Southward requested to be relieved of his 'A' team coaching duties to allow him to concentrate on scouting and youth development work. The man left to pick up the pieces was former Great Britain player Tommy Bishop, a tough scrum-half with a reputation to match, who had spent the last 12 years in Australia.

He faced the monumental task of lifting the club from the foot of the First Division where they were lodged with a paltry four points and the worst scoring record in the division.

His stormy reign at the club started with the announcement that he was going to make the players' lives hell. Those who didn't like it were rapidly shown the door.

"Winning is not everything, it's the only thing," said the straight-talking Bishop.

As a scrum-half with St Helens, Bishop won 15 Great Britain caps in the

Sixties, before playing for Sydney club Cronulla. After four years at Cronulla, he was tempted to Brisbane, where he began his coaching career and carved his name in Australian folklore. He further enhanced his reputation as a coach when he moved to Wollongong in New South Wales to take the Illawarra representative side unbeaten through their Caltex Country Championship-winning season. He also coached North Sydney in 1979, before completing his stint in Australia at his first club, Cronulla, the following year.

Paul had harboured hopes of being given the Town coach's job again, and was left disillusioned at the appointment of Bishop. The fiery Lancastrian's arrival at Derwent Park signalled the end of Paul's second spell with the club and the end of an era.

His career as one of the game's most accomplished full-backs had coincided with one of Rugby League's finest eras but, at the age of 39, Paul knew he could not go on forever. Ending his playing days at Workington had been the perfect way to bring the curtain down on his career. His inspirational leadership had helped them to their biggest triumph of the modern era when they won the 1977 Lancashire Cup.

However, there was to be one last roll of the dice, when, out of the blue, came a telephone call from Reggie Parker, the former Great Britain tour manager. Parker, chairman of Blackpool Borough, was on the lookout for some much-needed experience for his side. He knew just the man for the job.

A TASK TOO TOUGH

EVEN at the age of 39, Paul's passion for Rugby League showed no signs of abating. He was only too happy to answer Blackpool's call for help. But, after only a handful of games for the Seasiders, he reluctantly decided to call it a day. The cartilage injury which had kept him out of the Workington team for several months before his departure was still troubling him, and prevented him from showing Blackpool fans the skills that had made him a star.

His injury had been monitored for several months by Merseyside sport injury specialist Austin O'Malley, who warned Paul there was not much mileage left in his knee. Two decades and 727 appearances in the front line of one of the toughest of games had taken their toll on his body. Bringing the curtain down on a glorious career was more difficult than any split-second decision he had ever had to make as captain on the field, but he knew he had to submit to the realities of the situation. Many sportsmen who had achieved such acclaim were left with unrealistic expectations of themselves, which meant they didn't know when it was time to retire. Paul was determined not to be like that. He had always vowed he would allow his career to grind to a halt in a dignified manner.

Over the following few months his time was taken up by the more mundane business of working as a joiner on the BNFL site at Sellafield.

Paul was determined his retirement from professional Rugby League was not going to mean the end of his fitness regime. He continued to be a familiar sight pounding along the beach at St Bees to prevent himself from going to seed with the onset of middle age. He kept abreast of news and developments at Workington Town. If Paul's two spells at Derwent Park had taught him anything, it was always to expect the unexpected.

Even he, however, could not have been prepared for the startling turn of events in July 1982 when the club announced the sacking of controversial coach Tommy Bishop, the man who had guided them back to the First Division. It was a job made in heaven for Paul, even though he had reservations about applying for a position he had already held once.

Bishop's coaching ability had won him a host of admirers during his colourful 18-month reign at Derwent Park but his abrasive, no-holds-barred approach earned him as many critics. On the field, he could pride himself on helping Town win promotion and, in doing so, they ended the season as the game's top points scorers, but off the field, the storm clouds had gathered. He clashed with referees, with opposing coaches and players, he sacked the club's official supporters' group and alienated many other fans. The final straw came at Oldham before Town's last match of the season when he had a bitter row with directors over a night out to celebrate promotion.

Phil Kitchin, Frank Foster and Swinton's Tom Grainey had all been mentioned as possible replacements for Bishop. While the guessing games continued in the pubs and clubs around Workington, the directors knew exactly who they wanted.

Announcing Paul's appointment, director Jack Atkinson explained: "We as a board feel that Paul is the natural choice for the task ahead which is to maintain First Division Rugby League here at Workington.

"In considering the applicants for the post we had to pick a man who was not only an experienced professional but who could also withstand the pressures of First Division Rugby League. We feel that Paul has those qualities."

After having guided the club to promotion in 1976 as player-coach, Paul was almost picking up where he had left off. But he had no illusions about the task ahead of him.

"It's a hell of a challenge but I'm really looking forward to it," he told Cumbria's evening paper, the *News & Star*.

Like Bishop, Paul warned the directors that success depended on the team being strengthened with at least two top-class forwards the key priority. He was anxious to establish a solid forward platform to give his backs plenty of possession during the new campaign. One of his first successes was to persuade unsettled prop Allan Rowley that he had a future at the club after lengthy loan spells away from Workington.

The problems at Derwent Park ran deeper than Paul had at first anticipated. He sensed he did not have the full support of certain directors. He also became increasingly aware that several players were far from happy with the board's choice of coach. This hurt him deeply, but he believed that even without their backing, if he could get his team to produce the right results on the pitch, he could win his critics round. As for the dissenting players, they were simply told that if they didn't want to play for the club, they could leave. Paul knew from personal experience that unhappy players were of no use to a team.

Town's shortcomings on the pitch manifested themselves early into the troubled season with a first-round 20-12 Lancashire Cup defeat against a very ordinary Barrow outfit. That disappointment was followed soon afterwards by a John Player Trophy second round defeat by a York side anchored firmly at the bottom of the Second Division.

The league picture was no better, but Paul doggedly picked up the pieces each week and soldiered on. His love of Rugby League and Workington Town were facing their stiffest test yet.

The rumblings from the boardroom grew louder. He decided that in a climate of unrest, he had taken the side as far as he could. The job had become simply too heavy a burden, but eventually the decision about whether to resign was taken out of his hands when he was called to a board meeting after a training session in December 1982.

Paul immediately knew his fate. After a brief discussion about the problems on the pitch, chairman Steve Williams informed him he was relieving him of his duties.

Paul cleared out his desk, before making a hasty departure from Derwent Park – at the same time trembling more than a little for his successor.

FROM CUMBRIA COAST TO GOLD COAST

FOR only the second time in more than 20 years, Paul found himself out of Rugby League. But he was determined to look forward. It was a considerably more pleasant prospect than the last five months had proved. The experience at Workington had disillusioned him and he knew it would take time before his relationship with the club could heal. And nothing could take away his love of the game.

Closely guided by Paul, his teenage son Gary was rising through the junior ranks at Kells. A robust loose forward, Charlton junior had inherited his father's enthusiasm and will to win. During his enforced break from the professional game, Paul would ferry Gary and his young team-mates to training and weekend matches and shout encouragement from the touchline with all the other proud fathers.

St Bees had been home to the Charlton family for nearly 10 years. It had been a haven of tranquillity and peace for Paul, shielding him from the pressures and demands of Rugby League. The villagers knew him simply as one of the locals, who would have the occasional pint and chat with them in the pub, the Oddfellows Arms, or they would see him running along the beach.

Although they were well aware of his achievements, he was never treated like a sports star who had played at the highest level for club and country. Paul would not have wanted it any other way. Such special attention would have embarrassed him, though he was always happy to chat about the game in general when he spent a Sunday lunchtime relaxing in the pub with landlord George Cornish and his regulars. But he missed the game. It had been his life for as long as he could remember and he still felt he had something to offer even if only in the amateur ranks. It would also provide him with the chance to brush up his coaching skills in case he was ever offered a return to the professional game.

He and George had often talked about the possibility of setting up an amateur team in St Bees, but were unsure if there would be enough interest. It was a small, sleepy village on the coast with a population of little more than 1,000 people. The nearby communities of Kells, Hensingham and Distington were steeped in the tradition of Rugby League but St Bees was different.

There was a football team, which played in the local Sunday

League, and a cricket team, but apart from that most sporting activity was confined to St Bees School, one of the country's leading fee-paying schools. It was almost unthinkable that a Rugby Union-playing public school, which boasted former England RU captain and British Lions star Peter Dixon as one of its old boys, would even consider allowing its pupils to play the tough 13-a-side code.

Undeterred, Paul and George, with the help of a small band of other enthusiastic locals, pressed ahead with their plans to set up an amateur team. A meeting was called at the pub, which attracted a better response than expected, and from it a committee was formed to oversee operations.

The next step was to attract players good enough to be able to compete with long-established clubs in Division Three of the Cumberland Rugby League. Paul placed an advert in *The Whitehaven News* appealing for new players and took the even bolder move of inviting pupils from St Bees School, through the board of governors, to attend training sessions. It wasn't long before enough players had been recruited to allow them to join the league.

The idea of a new Rugby League team in the village was not to everyone's liking. At first, the soccer team opposed any plans to share their home at the Adams recreation ground in the village. Months of careful persuasion followed before the football team finally relented, but with a list of conditions. One of those was that the Rugby League team had to install a new drainage system to the field, which was susceptible to flooding in winter.

Money was tight but the committee contained a number of local tradesmen, like Paul and builder Tony Moorhouse, who were prepared to give up their free time to carry out the labouring work. Through his job, Paul heard that BNFL were selling a number of portable shower rooms cheaply. The army of volunteers clubbed together to buy one. Because there was no electricity to drive the shower unit, one of the villagers, Tom Hughes, a fitter at an engineering firm, suggested buying an old generator, which he would repair to working order.

Until work was completed at the Adams recreation ground, St Bees played at the County Ground in Whitehaven, near to the Recreation Ground.

The first season was a huge success. Led by their evergreen 42-year-old player-coach, they won promotion at the first attempt after being crowned Cumberland ARL Division Three champions.

The long break from professional Rugby League had also provided Paul with time to think about personal objectives rather than career goals. Ever since he had toured Australia with the Great Britain team in

1974, he had carried with him a dream of going out to live there. The country, the people and their culture had captivated Paul. He admired the Australian players' strong will to win, their discipline and their laid-back attitude off the field.

In 1985 he had returned for a huge reunion party with the rest of the Lions squad, and the following year he and Lillian had spent a month there on holiday. It had been Lillian's first visit and she too had fallen in love with the country as they toured hundreds of miles, meeting a number of former professionals.

Paul had several close friends who had emigrated Down Under, including his one-time Salford team-mate Peter Banner, who lived at Surfer's Paradise on the Gold Coast, where he ran a tour business. Banner's brother-in-law Rob was manager of The Tiki Hotel, where the couple stayed during their holiday. They had also met up with Paul's former Great Britain colleague Mike Stephenson, who had been settled in Australia with his family for more than 10 years since going out to play for Penrith in 1973.

Stephenson, who was working as a TV commentator on ABC, had organised the Lions reunion the year before.

"You should get yourselves out here, you'd love it", he had told Paul and Lillian.

Lillian shared her husband's wanderlust, and soon what had started as a dream became a real possibility. Melanie was 16 and had just left school. Gary was working as a lorry driver at Sellafield. Both shared their parents' enthusiasm for starting a new life in Australia. The support of the children was the deciding factor. In early 1987 Paul and Lillian put the wheels in motion by applying for visas.

★ ★ ★

The flight had seemed never-ending. Stepping on to the hot tarmac at Sydney gave Paul the chance at last to stretch his legs. It was only when he glanced at his watch that he realised how long the journey had taken. It brought home to him just how far from home he was. Under the terms of the visa, Paul had to arrive in Australia by May. It had seemed right for Paul to travel out alone, find a job and somewhere to live, before Lillian, Gary and Melanie flew out to be with him. They still had to sell their home in Cumbria, and it would be much simpler with Lillian there to oversee the sale.

As he collected his luggage and his bag of carpenter's tools and made his way from the bustling airport, Paul couldn't help but feel alone. It would be a tough few months in a new place without his family.

His thoughts were suddenly interrupted by a cry of "G'day mate", and he turned to see Stephenson grinning broadly as he leaned out of a car window.

The pair had known each other since the early Seventies when Stephenson was playing for Dewsbury and Paul was at Salford. They had also been team-mates during the 1972 World Cup. Stevo's home in Sydney was to be Paul's base for a few days, before he would move on to Coolangatta on the Gold Coast, to stay with Peter Banner.

Through Banner, Paul was introduced to Barry Roberts, a former Bolton Wanderers footballer, whose father-in-law Ted Manchip owned a flat above his house in Palm Beach. Ted, a Welshman, and his wife Gwynne were happy for Paul to rent it until his family arrived when they would buy a house of their own.

Paul's next step was to find work. After sifting through the situations vacant in the local paper, he began work as a carpenter for a building firm. It paid good money, which enabled him to send cheques home to Lillian.

There were times when he felt desperately lonely with his family on the other side of the world. To help lift the gloom of the long evenings on his own, he joined the Coolangatta touch rugby team, which played in a midweek league. It was a good chance to get out, meet new friends and have a bit of fun.

It was still a relief when in October, British Airways flight 71000 touched down at Sydney Airport, and he saw Lillian, Gary and Melanie walking across the tarmac towards him.

A CHIP OFF THE OLD BLOCK

WHILE Paul had been away, Gary's career had continued to blossom in the West Cumbrian amateur ranks. After leaving St Bees, where he had played under his father's wing, he spent a season playing in a higher division in the Cumberland League for Egremont Rangers. The move had done him good and he had developed into a strapping loose forward. Like many youngsters living in West Cumbria, Gary had never even considered soccer. The oval ball always held more appeal.

Unlike Paul, Gary stood over 6ft tall but, like his father, he wasn't afraid to go in where it hurt. His no-holds-barred style had earned him representative honours for BARLA, the organisation which runs amateur Rugby League.

The 20-year-old had been working at Sellafield, the biggest employer in Cumbria but, like his parents and younger sister, he was keen to experience a new way of life in Australia. Gary was also interested in playing for an Australian side and was keen to try to get fixed up with a club as soon as he got there.

Inevitably, people took more than a passing interest in him as soon as they discovered he was the son of a Great Britain international.

"You'll never be as good as your dad", he was constantly reminded but it didn't bother him. Like many sons of famous fathers, he was proud of his dad but wanted to do things his own way. He had no reservations about being in his father's shadow and was also level-headed enough to know he would never repeat his achievements. Paul was a constant source of encouragement to Gary and was always on hand for advice but he allowed him the space to make his own way in the game.

Paul had heard about a new club in New South Wales, the Gold Coast Giants. He told Gary they were looking for players. Gold Coast Giants were a new team just taking off in the New South Wales Premiership, along with Newcastle Knights and Brisbane Broncos. As part of their recruitment drive for the new season, which was only four months away, The Giants were holding a weekend of trials.

It attracted a massive response and competition for the 42 places was fierce, many of Gary's rivals being players with first grade Sydney experience. He knew it would be a feather in his cap to be selected, and would stand him in great stead if he ever decided to pursue a professional career back in England.

The trials were staged during the weekend under the watchful eyes of coaches Bob McCarthy and Malcolm Clift. The players got a chance to press their claims in 20 minute bursts, before they were substituted to give others a chance. At the end of the second day the players were all assembled on the pitch, while the names of the successful trialists were read out.

There was a hush as the players stood anxiously waiting for McCarthy to deliver his verdict. By the time he reached the 40th name, Gary was already convinced his hopes had been dashed. But, before there was time for the disappointment to sink in, his name was read out as one of as one of the Gold Coast's new recruits.

Apart from a few early pangs of homesickness, the Charlton family slowly began to settle into the Australian way of life. The sunshine of Sydney was a welcome change to the cold, damp, wintry conditions they had left behind in England. The cramped flat above Ted and Gwynne's house had served its purpose. Living there had given them time to adjust to their new surroundings until they found their feet.

It also meant they could wait until the money from the sale of their house in England came through before they began house-hunting. When the money was transferred to their Australian bank account, they found a newly-built bungalow in Elanora. The three bedroomed, modern detached property in a pretty suburb of Queensland cost $89,000. Their stay so far in Australia had seemed like an extended holiday. Now having a home of their own made them feel more settled. They loved their new lifestyle so much that Paul and Lillian decided to apply for dual British and Australian citizenship.

Paul was still working as a carpenter on the building site, and Lillian found a job with a timeshare company, which provided her with some independence and the chance to make new friends of her own. Melanie began working as an apprentice hairdresser. When he wasn't playing rugby, Gary worked as a dry-liner.

It wasn't long before Paul himself was also back in Rugby League. Tugan were a small club playing in Australia's Group 18, which offered the players a high standard of rugby. Paul went to watch them train one evening and asked coach Gerry O'Neill if he could join the club, with the prospect of perhaps playing the occasional second team game.

Even though he was 47, he had the fitness of a man half his age and knew he would still be capable of making the odd appearance just to satisfy his enthusiasm for the game.

He decided to keep his true age and identity hidden from O'Neill and his new club. He preferred to be anonymous and just be one of the lads for a change, rather than let them know he was a former Great Britain full-back, who had toured their country 14 years earlier. He was also afraid they might think he was bragging if he revealed exactly who he was and would perhaps treat him differently.

The following week he was named in the reserve team to face Southport. Paul rolled back the years and turned in an impressive performance.

Tugan were desperately short of players, thanks to an injury crisis. The first team was stretched almost to breaking point and they needed a couple of second team players to play as substitutes in their game against Southport's first team that afternoon. O'Neill asked Paul if he felt up to another game in the space of a few hours.

He was required only for the final 25 minutes to play on the wing. At full-time, he was waved over to the touchline by O'Neill, who had been engaged in an animated conversation with three Southport officials.

As he got closer, Paul overheard one of the Southport representatives telling O'Neill bluntly: "That ex-Great Britain international is not eligible to play for your first team because he hasn't played enough reserve matches".

His secret was out. There was no escape, and he had to come clean.

When O'Neill left Tugan, Paul applied for the vacant post, but missed out to Penrith player Warren Fenton. However, Fenton promoted Paul to assistant coach in charge of the second team

Meanwhile, Gary had enjoyed a successful season back in Britain with Hull Kingston Rovers during the Australian off-season. He had initially joined Sheffield Eagles after being contacted in Australia by their coach Gary Hetherington. After only six games, Hull KR, playing a division higher than Sheffield in the Stones Bitter Championship, moved in to sign him. The following season, his two-year contract with the Gold Coast Giants ended, and Gary again returned to Britain to play with his home town team, Whitehaven.

His powerful frame equipped him perfectly to cope with the game's bone-crunching tackles. In Rugby League there is a fine line between hard, uncompromising play and foul play. Gary's full-blooded, wholehearted approach to the game regularly brought him into conflict with referees. Charlton junior was the sort of player his own team's followers loved, but the opposing team's supporters loved to hate. But nothing could have prepared him for the vilification that followed an incident with Castleford's £145,000-rated stand-off Graeme Steadman during a Regal Trophy match in December 1989.

Steadman, ironically a friend and former Gold Coast Giants teammate of Gary, suffered a broken cheekbone and nose in the collision, which kept him out of the game for more than two months. Gary was sent off for what the referee considered to be a late, high challenge, but the repercussions went much further than him being sent for an early bath.

Whitehaven coach Eric Fitzsimmons suspended Gary indefinitely on the strength of a TV recording. The matter was referred to a Rugby League disciplinary committee. The incident came at a time when the game was cracking down on poor discipline. With Fitzsimmons refusing to offer any support, the outlook appeared bleak. But he could never have imagined just how badly things would turn out. The disciplinary committee decided to make an example of him and banned him indefinitely. They stressed it was not a life ban but one which effectively had no limit.

David Howes of the RFL warned: "A sine die ban is a rare occurrence and, in recent years, has only been inflicted on players hitting referees."

Gary was left distraught. 1990 had been an unhappy year for the Charlton family. News had reached them in Australia of the death of Paul's mother, Josephine. She had passed away peacefully, a victim of the respiratory problems which had afflicted her all her life.

Meanwhile, the news of Gary's ban stunned Paul and Lillian. They felt shock and disbelief that their son should be treated this way. Gary immediately decided he would appeal against the ban, even though he knew it would be a long process. Paul and Lillian were right behind him. Gary needed his family's support as he began the long, painful fight to clear his name. It was time for the Charltons to return to England.

FAMILY FORTUNES

AS his enforced exile from the game continued, Gary became increasingly convinced that he had been made a scapegoat as part of the Rugby League disciplinary crackdown. Paul shared his son's suspicions but it went much deeper than the family loyalty anyone might have expected from a devoted father. There were three other high-profile cases which backed their claim of inconsistencies in dealing with offenders.

Of those similar cases to go before the sport's disciplinary committee around the same time, the players received far lighter sentences than the one meted out to Gary. One player received an eight week ban, another 11 weeks and a third a 12 week suspension. One of those cases involved Widnes star Paul Moriarty, who stood accused of breaking the jaw of Oldham prop Hugh Waddell. The Welshman had escaped with a short ban.

Gary would never have considered himself a campaigner for justice but on this occasion, he felt he had no choice and launched an appeal to have his ban lifted.

Watching the proceedings carefully was Cameron Bell, the coach of Carlisle Border Raiders. The New Zealander had breathed new life into Carlisle, and the club was enjoying its most successful period since the heady days of promotion to the top flight in 1982.

Bell, father of Wigan captain Dean Bell, had been a big admirer of Gary since the player's time at Whitehaven, just as he had been of his father during his playing days. Now the highly-respected Kiwi was prepared to put his own reputation on the line to offer Gary a lifeline back into the game if the Rugby League authorities were prepared to give him a second chance at the age of 23. He had given Gary the opportunity to get back into shape by joining in the training sessions at Gillford Park, home of the Raiders. All he lacked was match fitness.

Speculation had been growing in the Press that his sine die ban would be lifted after ten months, but it still came as a surprise when, in November 1990, Gary was informed that he would be allowed to put the past behind him. Both he and Paul were still angry that they had been cast adrift by Whitehaven, but it was time for any bitterness to be forgotten. It was time to get back to the serious business of Rugby League and a new challenge with Carlisle Border Raiders.

The worry and anxiety failed to dent Gary's enthusiasm for the game or his confidence in maintaining the aggressive edge to his style of play. The question as to whether Carlisle's bold gamble would succeed was answered emphatically as Charlton junior went on to become one of the key members of their team. Bell liked Gary's whole-hearted approach. He saw him not just as a second-rower but as a high-impact utility player, who would add a new dimension and some much-needed depth to his small squad.

Bell had arrived at Carlisle a year earlier, having coached Manukau to domestic cup success in New Zealand and guided Auckland to wins over the touring Great Britain and Australian teams. His son Dean, who played for Wigan and the Kiwi international side, had started his own English career with Carlisle, cementing his links with the Border city by marrying a local girl. It seemed the ideal place for Bell senior to open a new chapter in his coaching career after just missing out on the New Zealand coach's job.

The club had just been boosted by the return of the Kiwi Test star Clayton Friend, who was lured back to the club after a seven-year spell playing with North Sydney. A master tactician with vast experience, Friend was actually Bell's nephew, and was equally at home at stand-off or scrum-half. He was a player capable of turning a game on his own. Friend's international experience was added to a team mixed with other New Zealand imports and locally-bred players, some of whom had learned their trade in the Cumbrian amateur ranks. Those players included the prolific and consistent try-scorer Kevin Pape, reliable full-back and goal-kicker Barry Vickers and powerful, strong-running prop Steve Brierley.

After underlining his potential in the Alliance team, Gary was promoted to the Carlisle first team and returned to where he had left off before his exclusion from the game.

Meanwhile, Paul became player-coach of Frizington in the Cumberland ARL, and, when he wasn't involved with his own team, he would watch Gary playing for Carlisle. His own professional playing career may have been long since finished but he was still fondly remembered by many as one of the all-time greats.

On one occasion he travelled to Yorkshire to watch the Challenge Cup tie between Carlisle and Castleford. After the game he was standing in a corridor chatting about the game to Raiders' officials. A queue of young children holding autograph books and match programmes was growing ever longer in anticipation of the Castleford players leaving the dressing room. As the wide-eyed youngsters swarmed around Lee Crooks and his team-mates, an elderly man standing nearby told them: "Don't bother with those bloody lot! This is the man whose autograph you want – he would have put that useless lot to shame!"

The children immediately abandoned the Castleford players and held their books out for Paul to sign.

Settling back into the English way of life had been much easier than Paul and Lillian thought. They had bought a plot of land in Mirehouse, Whitehaven, where Paul was busy building the new family home.

He had got to know his son's coach well. He and Cameron Bell shared a common philosophy on the game, and there had been an instant rapport between them. Bell was convinced Rugby League was a poorer game without Paul's knowledge and experience, and was keen to bring him on board at Carlisle Border Raiders in some capacity.

Bell was assisted at Carlisle by Dave Robley, who had made his name as a top Rugby Union coach with Cumbrian club Aspatria. Seeking a fresh challenge after leading Aspatria to a record 12 county championships in just 15 years, Robley switched codes and joined Carlisle as a conditioner, aimed at improving the stamina and fitness of the players.

But what Carlisle needed was an Alliance League coach to groom young players and teach them good habits, as well as bring out the best in their current second team players. It was vital to their future well-being because they did not have the finances to go out and pay big money for players. Carlisle were dependent on the talent from west coast hot-beds like Whitehaven, Workington and Maryport. From his experience in the amateur ranks and his standing in the game, Paul was the ideal man to strengthen their link with West Cumbria.

After a break of nine years he was looking forward to returning to the professional game with a challenging role. But Paul could not have realised just how challenging his new job would sometimes be, when, in September 1991, at the age of 49, he came out of retirement to play in the Alliance side.

He still paid almost as much attention to his personal fitness as he did in his playing hey-day and he didn't hesitate when injury problems forced him to step in at stand-off. The team responded to his enthusiasm and motivation by recording their best win of the season when they beat a strong Swinton side 22-16.

Off the field, Carlisle were a club beset with financial problems. There simply weren't enough fans going through the turnstiles. The biggest trauma for chairman Alan Tucker and his board of directors came in 1993 when the club received a winding-up order. It involved an unpaid VAT bill of nearly £10,000, and they only narrowly managed to avert disaster. Being a Rugby League director in the modern game almost by definition meant the board had to put their hands in their own pockets to bale the club out of another crisis.

But the rescue was not without its victims. The financial problems meant the club had to make cutbacks and one involved the coaching staff. Bell was left with the unhappy decision of choosing between his assistant Dave Robley and Paul, his second team coach. With a heavy heart, Bell had to inform his Alliance team coach that his services were no longer required.

But Paul's goodbye to Carlisle Border Raiders was not for long.

BACK IN THE HOT SEAT

PROFESSIONAL adaptability was never a problem for Paul. Although he would have loved the opportunity to remain involved with a full-time Rugby League club, he jumped at the chance to become coach of Lowca, a small amateur team in West Cumbria.

His enthusiasm for the game was as strong as ever, although at times it was tested to the limit. There had been problems behind the scenes at Lowca, which resulted in virtually the whole team quitting the club. At Paul's first training session, only six players turned up. When it came to the opening game of the season against Hensingham, he had only 11 players from which to pick 13!

At the age of 52 he had to come out of retirement again and play in a team which had started a man short and was then reduced to 11 when John Allan was forced to leave the action with an ankle injury. Not surprisingly, Lowca were hammered 88-0. But by mid-season the club's fortunes had been transformed spectacularly.

The presence of an ex-Great Britain star acted like a magnet for local players. Former players returned to the fold. New ones asked if they could join, and soon a squad of more than 20 players had been assembled. It wasn't long before they started winning games, and three victories in their last four matches ensured they managed to stave off what had looked like almost certain relegation.

The 1994-95 season began with hopes high that Lowca could build on the hard work Paul and the players had put in the previous year, and possibly challenge for honours in both the Cumberland ARL and in the cup competitions. But a phone call from Carlisle Border Raiders chairman Alan Tucker changed all that.

Border Raiders were in turmoil on and off the field. The club had a chequered history and recurring financial worries meant its future was even more unclear. Cameron Bell had left the club at the end of the previous season to return to New Zealand, and had been replaced by former Oldham, Leeds and Great Britain prop Hugh Waddell.

But Waddell had been unable to inspire confidence among the players or directors. After fewer than six months in charge at Gillford Park, he was sacked in December 1994. His dismissal was prompted by a damaging 16-30 defeat by Dewsbury, the latest in a string of disappointing league results in which Carlisle won only three out of nine games.

Waddell was invited to remain at the club as a player. Paul was handed the coach's job and the responsibility of trying to revive their flagging Second Division campaign midway through the season. While Waddell contemplated his future as a player, his parting shot as coach perhaps summed up the size of the task Paul faced.

"It is not a new coach Carlisle need, it is new players", he said.

"Does the chairman Alan Tucker think players will stop falling off tackles because there is a new coach? Does he think players will suddenly develop astronomical pace so that when we make a break they can score tries? Or does he think we need new players, as I've been saying since I've been here? I wish Paul all the best – it is a hell of a job. But if he doesn't get assistance from the board he can forget about it."

With a lot of hard work, Carlisle's new coach began the job of trying to turn things around on what made a shoestring budget look like the crown jewels. They ended a traumatic 1994-95 season third from bottom in the Second Division with only Highfield and Barrow below them but the seeds of improvement had been sown.

Paul's inspirational leadership was built on a stubborn refusal to accept the limitations of his players. He was convinced that with improved discipline and fitness, he could bring the best out of them and make them win games. It didn't go down well with all of them. A few felt that because he had been a great player himself surrounded by equally big stars, his demands of them were unrealistic. But Paul had no time for negative thinkers and his first job was to introduce a tough disciplinary code at the club.

It was how he had been taught as a player and he expected the same high standards from his players. A notice was pinned up in the dressing room outlining the new rules his players were expected to follow. They were warned they would be fined for being late for the bus, not wearing either tracksuits or club blazer, shirt, collar and tie for away games, having dirty boots, being sin-binned or sent off.

Players were also instructed that they had to be at the ground an hour-and-a-half before kick-off. If they were five minutes late they would be fined and if they were more than five minutes late, they would be relegated to the substitutes' bench. Fines would be doubled for regular offenders.

Although it was tough, Paul was anxious to ensure it was not an oppressive regime. The fine money was used to buy steaks, sausages and soft drinks for barbecues after Saturday morning training sessions. He would never abuse his power as coach to dominate or manipulate but to encourage players to release their full potential.

He was also fiercely loyal to his men. Although he would not hesitate to reprimand them for poor performances behind closed doors, he would never tolerate anyone else criticising them, whether it be the chairman or directors. It created a good atmosphere and strong team spirit which was to help pull the club through some of the roughest times during his three-year reign.

Paul radiated a positive personality and his players found his enthusiasm for the game infectious. There was a new-found air of optimism as Carlisle prepared for his first full season in charge.

On the recommendation of former coach Cameron Bell, they had just recruited Tane Manihera, a stand-off, who had toured Britain in 1993 with the Junior Kiwis squad. Manihera, who had been playing in New Zealand's Lion Red competition, was handed a free role in the side and his game began to flourish in the extra space of English Rugby League. He succeeded in bringing a touch of class to the Raiders team, which already boasted talented Australian hooker Danny Russell.

Russell had started his career with Manly in the Winfield Cup, the world's toughest Rugby League competition. His leadership qualities had prompted Paul to appoint him assistant coach.

Paul had also managed to persuade goal-kicking supremo Willie Richardson out of retirement. The silver-haired full-back's all-action style belied his veteran status.

Gary Charlton was revelling in the responsibility of being made captain by his father and Matt Lynch, a recruit from Rugby Union, had taken to the 13-man game with remarkable ease.

The side, which had managed only eight victories during the whole of the previous season, were transformed into a team capable of making a serious attempt to win promotion. By the end of November, Carlisle had recorded 10 successive wins and were topping the Stones Bitter Third Division, playing a brand of free-flowing rugby not seen at Gillford Park for some time.

The highlight of Carlisle's rejuvenation came on November 11 when they confounded even their most loyal supporters by dumping Castleford out of the Regal Trophy. They had done well to dispose of Hunslet in the previous round, but no one had given them a serious chance of making the last eight of the competition at the expense of their illustrious Yorkshire opponents. The never-say-die attitude instilled into them by their ambitious coach had helped prove everyone wrong.

Russell's tackling, kicking and astute distribution laid the foundation for the victory but it was a fine all-round team performance which earned Raiders the greatest result in their 14-year history. Carlisle's exhausted players tackled for their lives until Mike "Bluey" Kavanagh's drop goal 15 minutes from time earned them a shock 19-18 second-round win.

Long after the final hooter, Castleford coach John Joyner sat distraught in the deserted stand his head in his hands, before walking disconsolately around the pitch trying to take in the enormity of it all. Meanwhile, in the clubhouse, Carlisle's celebrations were in full swing.

Carlisle's Regal Trophy campaign ended with a quarter-final defeat against Leeds, but their brave run had won them a host of new admirers. The huge progress they had made was also reflected in their top-five finish in the league. Strong foundations had been laid for future success.

Coach Ike Southward leads out Workington Town's 1977 Lancashire Cup side, followed by captain Paul Charlton. Southward's former Great Britain colleague Vince Karalius leads out Wigan.

Paul and Town coach Ike Southward shake hands with Rugby League officials. Town won the Lancashire Cup at Wilderspool, beating Wigan 16-13.

Disaster strikes for Paul as he severely damages knee ligaments during the Lancashire Cup final, which forces him out of the action.

Les Gorley and Derek Watts attempt to win the ball with Paul closely watching developments.

Paul leads the victorious Workington team up the steps to lift the Lancashire Cup. He is followed by big Jim Mills.

It's ours! Paul holds the Lancashire Cup aloft. Left to right: Paul, Ray Wilkins, Billy Pattinson, player obscured, John Risman.

Nearly 5,000 fans travelled to Wilderspool to cheer on their heroes in the 1977 Lancashire Cup final. "When I stood up there and saw all the blue and white scarves, a lump came to my throat", said Paul.

Workington president Tom Mitchell holds the Lancashire Cup. Directors George Graham (far left) and Jack Atkinson also join in the celebrations, while Peter Gorley (right) is wearing Mitchell's hat.

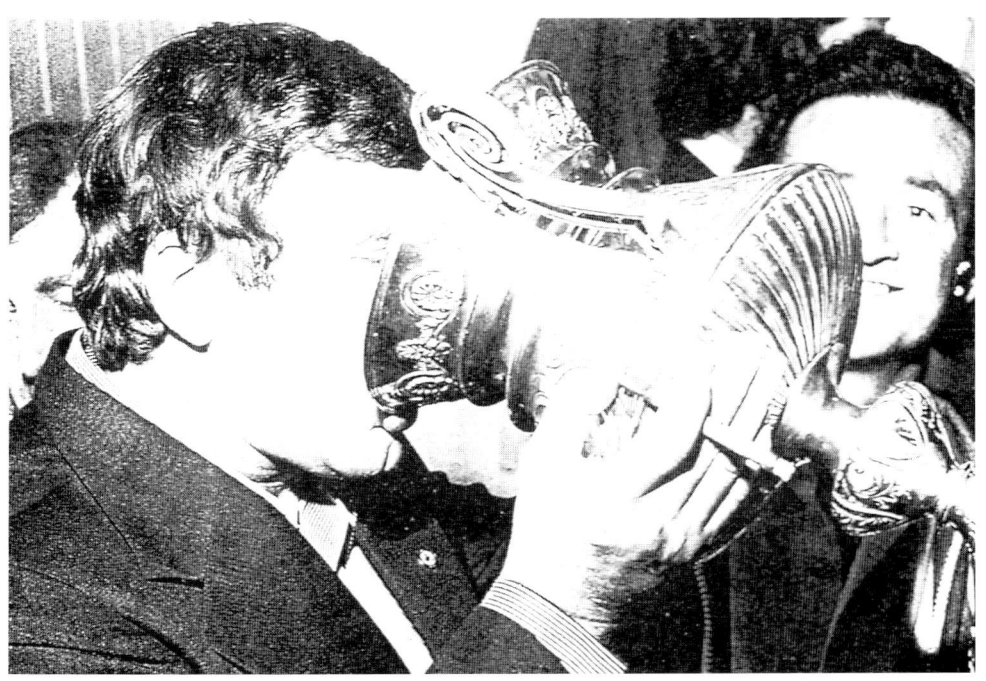

A champagne moment for coach Ike Southward as he has a drop of bubbly from the Lancashire Cup watched by conditioner Andy Key.

Mayor of Workington Bob Spedding (left) and the Mayor of Allerdale Arthur Robinson welcome Town's Cup-winning team at a civic reception. Left to right: Ray Wilkins, Ian Wright, Les Gorley, Bill Pattinson, Alan Banks, Ian Hartley, Andy Key, Peter Gorley, Ike Southward, John Risman and Paul.

The victorious team. Back (left to right): Ken Groves, Bill Pattinson, David Atkinson, David Collister, Paul, Alan Banks, Les Gorley, Eddie Bowman, Peter Gorley, John Risman. Front: Ray Wilkins, Ian Wright, Boxer Walker, Ian Hartley.

Workington's Wigan Sevens winning team of 1978. Back (left to right): Bill Pattinson, Alan Banks, Ian Hartley, Iain MacCorquodale, George Graham (director). Front: Boxer Walker, Paul Charlton and Ian Wright.

Boxer Walker sets off in search of the try-line with Paul close behind. Boxer played 191 games for Workington, scoring 53 tries and two goals.

Despite the advancing years, Paul still worked hard at maintaining his fitness. Here in the autumn of his career, he gives Workington fans a reminder of the pace and skills which once made him the world's costliest full-back.

Two Workington Town stars from different eras, Gus Risman and Paul Charlton. Risman won 17 Great Britain caps, while Paul won 19 and holds the honour of being the most capped Town player.

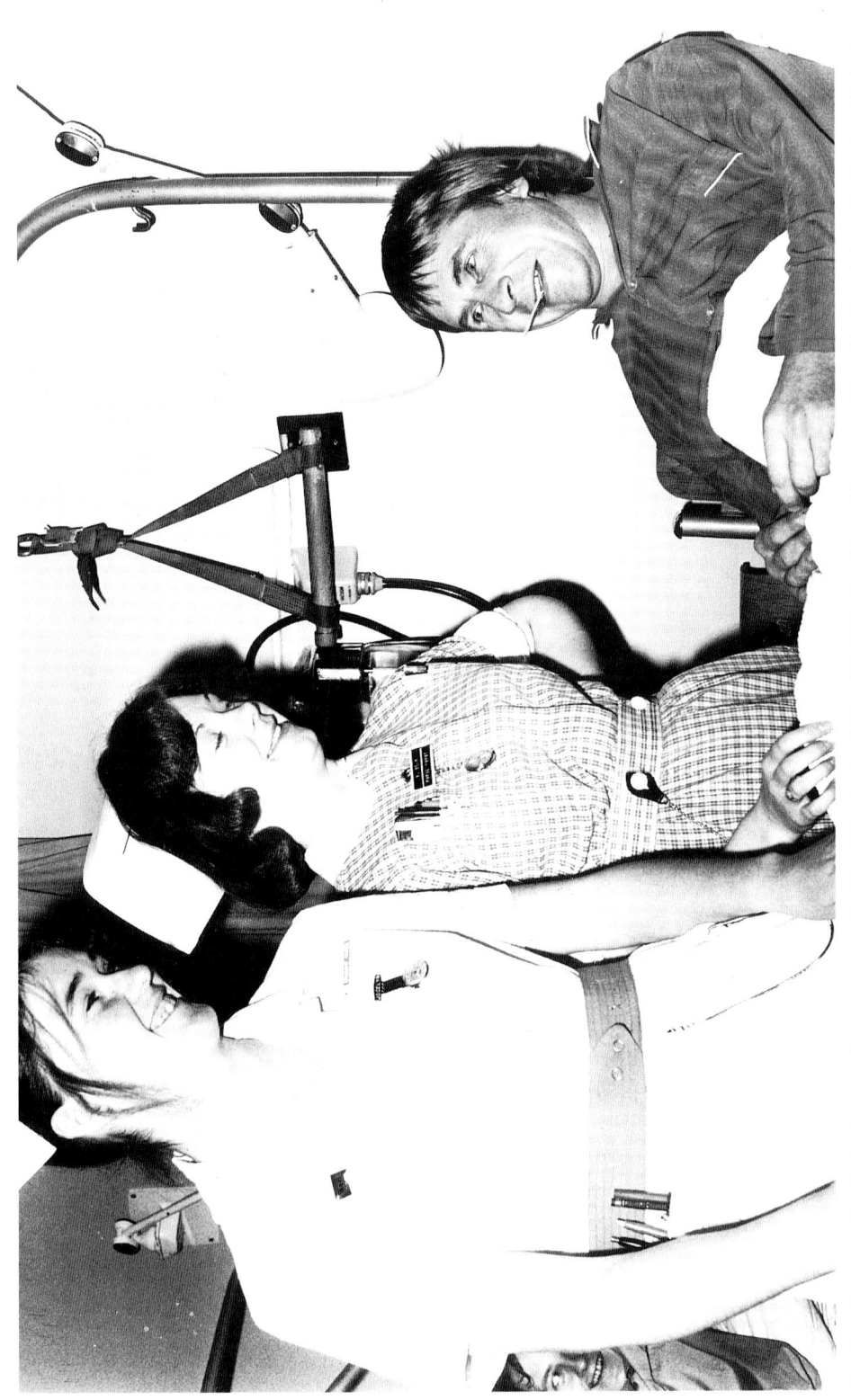

Paul receives some tender loving care from nurses at the West Cumberland Hospital following his cartilage operation. The knee injury finally forced him to retire in 1981 after 718 full appearances, scoring 223 tries and 89 goals.

New Zealander Cameron Bell takes shelter from the English weather. The former Carlisle Border Raiders coach appointed Paul as his Alliance team coach in 1991.

Carlisle Border Raiders trio Tane Manihera, Danny Russell and Richard Henare celebrate winning the Stones Bitter Third Division team of the month under Paul's guidance. As coach, Paul twice led them to the brink of promotion.

The Charlton name lives on. Paul's son Gary has enjoyed a successful Rugby League career of his own with Carlisle Border Raiders and Whitehaven. On the right is his Whitehaven team-mate Lee Kiddie.

SO NEAR, YET SO FAR

PAUL had arrived at Gillford Park with a reputation for being physically and mentally tough. Players grimaced when they heard stories about how their fitness-fanatic coach would put himself through punishing training routines. They knew he would expect the same from them. The start of pre-season training was always greeted with dread. They feared he would stretch them to the limit.

Paul was also convinced recovery from injuries and illness was a case of mind over matter. His tried-and-trusted remedy for a cold was to wrap up in three jumpers and sweat it out by cycling up the Cumbrian fells or jogging along the sand dunes. Players rolling around on the pitch clutching themselves in agony after a tackle got used to cold comfort from their coach.

Paul's toughness was displayed when he was admitted to hospital to have a cartilage operation, a painful procedure which required a general anaesthetic. Most people would have taken a week to recuperate. Two hours after the operation he discharged himself from Carlisle's Cumberland Infirmary. At 6pm he had his players rubbing their eyes in disbelief as he hobbled on to the training pitch on crutches to put them through yet another gruelling session.

Paul was cautious about making bold predictions about his side's chances of promotion as they prepared to kick off the 1997 season. He was more than satisfied with the spirit of determination among his players, who had answered his call to arms without a trace of self-doubt.

But the previous two seasons had proved beyond doubt that his squad desperately lacked the strength in depth to sustain a serious promotion push over six gruelling months.

The previous season had heralded the dawning of a new era for the game with the introduction of summer rugby. Carlisle had underlined the progress they were making under Paul's leadership by finishing fourth.

He had to rely on a small squad with few experienced players in reserve. It took only a couple of injuries or suspensions to disrupt the whole season and leave their promotion dream in tatters. Paul was constantly reminded by directors that money was not available to buy success. Coming so close to winning promotion in the last two seasons and the memorable victory over Castleford had not inspired supporters. The club was only just surviving on gates of not many more than 400.

There was also frequent unrest among the players about unpaid wages.

Paul's other concern was that several key players, instead of resting during the close season, had chosen to play Rugby Union. They were still fresh for the start of the Rugby League season but Paul was convinced they would struggle to stay the course. It was frustrating to think that no matter how well prepared they were for the coming season, there were so many factors out of Paul's control. Nevertheless, he unfailingly managed to make the best of the situation.

A confidence boosting 22-14 home win over Batley got the season under way. The game was to give plenty of pointers as to how the coming months would go.

Pre-season signing Darryl Menzies, who had stepped off a flight from New Zealand only 17 hours earlier, began his Carlisle career in what was to become typical style, scoring tries from his first two chances.

In Menzies and fellow winger Gary Ruddy, whom Paul had signed from the amateur ranks in South Cumbria, Raiders boasted Division Three's two best try-scorers. They were to prove their worth to the side in a match against Prescot when the pair set a new club record by scoring five tries each in Carlisle's 15-try massacre of the Merseysiders.

Stand-off Jamie Stevens, a young Maori representative, was living up to his potential. The club had also managed to unearth a gem in teenager Darren Holt. The youngster was an anachronism – a Rugby League playing former public school boy, who was proving to be a top class replacement for Danny Russell, who, at the turn of the year, had joined Huddersfield Giants.

By June, Carlisle were still occupying second place but two disastrous games were to destroy their promotion dream.

In three dramatic minutes against Leigh Centurions, they were changed from promotion favourites to rank outsiders after the cruellest of refereeing decisions.

With Carlisle leading 8-6 in the tightest of games, forward Jonathan Hughes stretched through several bodies to touch down beneath the posts. Referee Paul Lee awarded the try. But as Raiders players celebrated, in-goal official Bob Southward told the referee that Hughes had grounded the ball after he had been held. Astonishingly, the referee chose not to believe the evidence of his own eyes and disallowed the try which would have given Carlisle a decisive 14-6 advantage.

As Carlisle's concentration was broken by the injustice of it all, Leigh took full advantage of uncharacteristic fumbles by Menzies and Willie Richardson to set up a 24-12 victory they hardly deserved.

The odds on Carlisle winning promotion began to lengthen. A

controversial encounter with Cumbrian neighbours Barrow ended with an impressive 32-6 victory but it was what happened in the game that proved to be the undoing of their season.

The strong rivalry between the two sides was graphically displayed by several bouts of fisticuffs. Forward Stuart Rhodes, playing against his former Barrow colleagues, was sent off for a second time in the season after a clash with Neil Measures. Rhodes was left facing a lengthy suspension, which was to make him a key absentee during his side's difficult run-in. To add to their problems, the bruising encounter also robbed Paul of the services of several players, who were left nursing injuries, while a few others, as their coach had predicted, began running out of steam.

By July the dream was over. Their last chance of promotion was mercilessly crushed in a devastating 66-28 defeat at the hands of Rochdale. Although they managed to score five tries and Ruddy grabbed a hat-trick for the second week running, Carlisle paid the price for defensive lapses and handling errors.

All Paul's fears had been realised. His players had again proved they were able to compete with any side in Division Two when they were able to field a strong side but, once injuries and suspensions began to take their toll, the squad lacked the strength in depth to compete. It had all conspired to wreck their promotion dream. In the end, only four points separated them from the promotion spots, which were taken by Hunslet and Rochdale. Carlisle were left once again to reflect on what might have been.

PASTURES NEW

PAUL put the telephone down and returned to the living room where Lillian was watching television.

"That was really strange", he said shaking his head as he sat down in the armchair.

"It was Alan Tucker on the phone. He says there's going to be a story in next week's newspaper that Cameron Bell is coming back to the club to replace me. But he says not to take any notice of it."

Paul could not get the phone call out of his head. It had been a confusing conversation and he kept turning it over and over in his mind. If none of it was true, as the Carlisle chairman had insisted, why had Bell told the local newspaper that he had been approached about the possibility of returning from New Zealand? It just didn't make sense.

Paul could not understand why Carlisle should want to get rid of him. He had done a good job on limited resources and had taken them agonisingly close to promotion. All he could do was wait until the story broke and see exactly what it said.

Paul picked up the newspaper and stared in disbelief. It was worse than he had anticipated.

"RAIDERS TURN TO KIWI CAMMY ONCE AGAIN," screamed the headline.

Bell, speaking from his home in New Zealand, confirmed that he had been approached by Tucker and admitted he would jump at the chance of a return.

"I do believe that, having looked at the side they had this year, with one or two extra players, I could take them to promotion", Bell was quoted as saying.

"Although we did very well with meagre finance when I was at the club, we did not do what I wanted, which was to get promotion. That is my desire now – to come back and finish off where I left."

Paul was stunned and hurt. It was the lowest point in his coaching career. He had given the job his full commitment. He had clocked up nearly 400 miles a week between Carlisle and his home in Whitehaven, combining the demands of coaching with a full-time job as a carpenter with Eden Council.

Carlisle insisted they were only exploring their options, as they were entitled to do. Rather than speaking out, Paul chose to keep a dignified silence. He was determined not to lose his integrity. He was left with the task of lifting his players' heads for the remaining Premiership games. He was certainly not going to leave them in the lurch.

Paul knew it would not be easy to focus their attentions on the game because they were not being paid. They had agreed to help out the cash-strapped club by waving their contract payments and win bonuses. Instead they were playing for just a share of the gate money. Paul had been touched by the support of his players who had deep respect for him.

But as the season ground to an end, both Paul and Carlisle Border Raiders were preparing for a change of direction. For some time Paul and Lillian had talked about the possibility of returning to Australia.

Both Gary and Melanie were grown up with families of their own and it was perhaps time for Paul and Lillian to pursue their own dreams. They had both felt at home in Australia and had never ruled out a return in the future. They still had many friends there and the fact they were both had dual citizenship, literally meant Australia was a second home.

It had often been a source of amusement to his players that Paul appeared to regard himself more as an Antipodean than an Englishman. Even his accent was a bizarre mixture of Australian and West Cumbrian. On one occasion Great Britain's prospects of beating the touring Australian side had been built up in the press. Paul remarked to Carlisle's Queensland-born hooker Danny Russell: "I can't believe the Poms think they're going to beat us!"

The uncertainty over his future at Gillford Park had made up Paul and Lillian's minds about emigrating. If he was asked to stay on, he could always simply return to Britain for the Rugby League season.

But behind-the-scenes there were dramatic developments at Carlisle. The job of sustaining Rugby League at Gillford Park on dwindling crowds had become an impossible task. Carlisle had always been a confirmed soccer city, and grass roots Rugby League was small and inconsequential by comparison.

Negotiations had been going on about the possibility of a merger between Carlisle and Barrow. Under the terms of the arrangement, the new club would be based at Barrow's Craven Park. It would be called Barrow Border Raiders and include the best players from both sides.

The decision was greeted with shock and dismay by Paul, his players and the club's small but loyal band of supporters. The union of two clubs 90 miles apart on the extreme fringes of Cumbria and the plan to stage all home games in Barrow effectively spelled the end of the professional game in Carlisle after 16 years of struggling in the Rugby League wilderness.

BACK TO THE FUTURE

THE hair is slightly greyer, the figure a little fuller and he may not be as fast with a ball in his hands, but Paul's enthusiasm for Rugby League is as strong as ever. The weather-beaten features are the tell-tale signs of a lifetime spent at the forefront of the game. At an age when most former players are content just to enjoy their memories, Paul is facing up to one of the biggest challenges of his career.

After his association with Carlisle Border Raiders ended in 1997, he and Lillian settled in Worongary, a suburb of the Gold Coast, just ten minutes from Surfer's Paradise. It was perhaps appropriate that Australia became his home as it was the country where he fulfilled his greatest ambition – playing for the touring British Lions.

Paul's career may have had more twists than a roller-coaster, but even he could not have expected the latest turn of events. Unknown to him, thousands of miles away back in Cumbria, there was unrest at Barrow Border Raiders. A question mark was hanging over the future of coach Stuart Wilkinson, who had been unable to guide the club to promotion.

Barrow began the 1998 season as promotion favourites after the team had been strengthened by the addition of a number of Carlisle players. They made a promising start and were topping the Second Division after three games. But their challenge for honours faded and they ended the season third bottom in the table with a record of eight wins, two draws and ten defeats.

Ironically, it had been Wilkinson who was given the job of coach ahead of Paul when Barrow and Carlisle merged the previous year. Despite that, Paul was still highly respected by Barrow directors and rumours began circulating that he could be offered a return to the game.

After a board meeting at the beginning of September, Wilkinson was told he would not be offered a new contract. A shortlist of three names was drawn up for the vacant coach's position, and it quickly became clear that Paul was top of the list.

Barrow directors knew that appointing a popular figure like Paul, who was still a big name in Rugby League, would go a long way to appeasing discontent among their long-suffering fans. Former Carlisle chairman Alan Tucker, a director at Barrow, conducted negotiations with Paul over the telephone.

Tucker later revealed to Carlisle's evening newspaper the *News & Star*: "Paul is a strong contender for the job.

"He is being considered but no decision has been made by either party. I have spoken to him and he would like to come back."

Days later Barrow chairman Alan Winward received a fax from Paul in Australia accepting their offer of a one year contract, with the option of a further year. The chance to return to the game was just too tempting for Paul to turn down. At a time of life when he perhaps thought Rugby League could offer him no further challenges, he has taken on one of the toughest jobs in the sport.

Since Frank Foster's ten year reign ended with the sack in 1983, Barrow have had 15 coaches. No one has stayed in the job longer than two years. After the glory years of the Fifties when they won the Challenge Cup in 1955, the club has enjoyed only fleeting success. For the last 15 years Barrow have struggled and attendances have started to dwindle.

Paul is under no illusions as to the size of the task ahead of him. But the potential of a club like Barrow has also not been lost on him. His ambition is to bring the good times back to Craven Park. He wants the team to play an attractive style of free-flowing rugby, which will lure the missing supporters back to the club.

"Barrow has been in the doldrums for too long and I think the club could have a future as good as its past", said Paul.

"The club is a sleeping giant and it is about time it woke up. There is the potential for a great following as it is the only team within a 40-mile radius.

"If we can get some good players on board and we all do our jobs properly, we can start getting the crowds back."

For many people, Paul is back where he belongs – at the heart of Rugby League.

Only time will tell if he can achieve the success with Barrow his drive and enthusiasm deserves.

There is one certainty, though, in his life. Paul Charlton was one of Cumbria's favourite sons and one of Rugby League's all-time greats.

TODAY'S GAME

PAUL Charlton is one of Rugby League's most respected figures.

The world's top full-back in his hey-day, he has played at the highest level, and was also a successful coach with Workington Town and Carlisle Border Raiders. In September 1998 he was appointed as the new coach of Barrow Border Raiders.

He has a strong philosophy on how the game should be played and believes not all the changes in the sport in recent years have been for the good.

Here he gives his views . . .

During my playing days men would go out on to the pitch and put their bodies on the line in the name of Rugby League. We risked serious injuries every time we went on the field from the constant punishment of playing against huge, hard men, who were afraid of losing.

There were no big-money contracts or sponsorship deals. We played for far less-worldly pleasures – comradeship and the thrill of winning.

If the players of my era were still playing today, they would be wealthy sports stars, who could be set up for life by playing the game they loved. Players of my generation earned peanuts, but it didn't matter one bit. The money was secondary. We went out to play Rugby League and we went out with a will to win.

The hunger just doesn't seem to be there in today's game. Although there are exceptions, some players just go out and think about the money they can make. That can only be bad for the game.

I don't believe in big contracts. I think there should be a loyalty bonus for players who stick with a club. They should be made to work for the money they make from the game.

Another big difference between my playing days and the modern era is the low profile today's players have, despite a much bigger media presence and the hype in sport.

When I was a youngster still dreaming of a career as a Rugby League player and during my own playing days, many of the men who pulled on a Rugby League shirt were household names, like Willie Horne, Gus Risman, Billy Ivison, Ike Southward, Alex Murphy and David Watkins. The list was endless. In comparison, today's Rugby League players are almost anonymous. There seem to be fewer and fewer big stars who can capture the public's imagination and raise the profile of the British game.

My favourite players today are the ones who can act as good

ambassadors for the game and help fill a stadium. Martin Offiah brings class and flair to the game, and he is one of the few players I would pay money to go and see. I played alongside many famous names as a player and he is a bit of a throwback to that era.

Shaun Edwards is also a cracking player. He can control and dictate the play. He's a typical cheeky scrum-half. His defence isn't as good as it should be and Shaun would probably be the first to admit that, but his ball skills are tremendous.

I am a big fan of London Broncos and I have followed their progress closely. I don't like following big all-star teams who are already successful. I take great pleasure in seeing a club start at the bottom and watch them climb to the top.

When I lived in Australia I was a fervent supporter of the Gold Coast Giants from the time they were first formed. The London Broncos remind me of them for their enthusiasm and spirit.

Coaching has also radically changed since I took my exams in the mid-Seventies. Tommy Thompson, who runs the Cumberland set-up with Phil Kitchin, was telling me that what they do with youngsters today is completely different. They still try to teach guys the skills of 25 years ago, but the other side of the coin is what you eat and what kind of work you should do in the gym.

I think that is something which is for the good of the game. It can only help players. If someone is working in an office all day and only training twice a week, they are not getting enough preparation for games. I've never been in a gym in my life but that's because I worked in a tough trade as a carpenter on a building site. If I had been in the forwards I would have had to build myself up, but as a full-back, doing that would have meant I would lose my speed. Instead of being a racing car, I would have ended up a juggernaut.

Today's game has gone soft and because of that a lot of the entertainment has been taken out. I think spectators like to see what I call a bit of "biff".

Every Test match I played in you could guarantee there would be a brawl after 10 minutes. The crowd would love it. A few big hits and a few punches were taken for granted. The game would then settle down and some great football would be played.

I am not condoning reckless play. Elbows should be kept out of the game and so should swinging arms. You don't need that in the game and people deserve to be punished. I feel that Greg McCallum, who was brought in to clean up the game, did a fair job but went overboard. Rugby League used to be a hard, physical contact sport. McCallum cut that out and encouraged referees to do the same.

We are left with this idea that any tackle above the chest area has to warrant 10 minutes in the sin-bin. There has to be a place in the game for good, hard, solid tackling. If someone is caught on the shoulder, the crowd is incensed and the player who has been tackled immediately complains. We have got people brain-washed into not knowing the difference between a high tackle and a fair tackle.

The Australians haven't changed their style over the years. They hit hard and they hit fair, but they hit between the rules. In the 1997 Test between Great Britain and Australia, Gordon Tallis, of Australia, was condemned because he was hitting hard and high, even though there was no malice in his actions. That has been taken out of the English game, and it should be brought back, not to the point of knocking people's heads off intentionally, but I feel referees should be more lenient with big-hitting players.

The modern game has definitely sped up around the play the ball area to try to make the game more entertaining. When I played we used the five yard rule. Now it has been taken back to 10 metres, which means there is less physical contact. Players have to be more athletic nowadays. That is not to say we didn't have skilful players, we did. We also had to think a lot faster when we got the ball in our hands because we had less time with it.

When it was first announced that a Super League was to be set up in Britain, I greeted the news with optimism. Like many people I thought it was a great idea. Now I feel that I made the wrong judgement. The day the Super League was set up, the game shot itself in the foot. They are still trying to get the bullet out, but it's too late. Too much damage has been done.

Australia fought against the Super League Down Under. I feel they were right to do that because it is now causing problems there too.

The gap between the haves and the have-nots in Rugby League is growing ever-wider. The vast amount of money which was brought into the game was not used properly. I believe it killed off sponsorship from other sources.

The game budgeted around the money they would receive from Sky, instead of trying to bring in money from other sources. Instead of using the money to develop the game in the right areas, they gave it to the players, who were only too quick to take it. I think every club was guilty of that. Clubs survived before Super League money, but now they can't survive because they don't have sponsorship.

I fear for the future of the small clubs in Britain and am worried they might disappear, as my old club Carlisle Raiders did. The future of the game depends on these smaller clubs because they act as feeders for the big teams. We can't afford to let them die.

I believe Carlisle's decision to merge with Barrow was all wrong. It spelled the end of professional Rugby League in that area. Carlisle is now an area with no Rugby League. That was destructive. People worked hard to introduce the game. They included Garry Schubert, Carlisle City Council's Rugby League development officer, who did a fantastic job in the schools.

There were some really talented young players coming through and the question now is this: Where do they go? The hard work Garry and others have done is in danger of going down the drain, and these good young players will be lost to the game. A 16-year-old who has a future as a Rugby League player would have to leave his home area to join a club. They may be reluctant to do that at an early age.

Carlisle had three teams at one stage. Now that is all gone. All the city has left is an amateur team, the St Nicholas Arms, but I hope perhaps one day Carlisle can start up another team through the Conference League.

The other big mistake we have made in Britain with summer Rugby League is allowing our players to play Rugby Union in the winter. It is an easy option for the player to make money but it does nothing to help the game of Rugby League.

Midway through the Rugby League season, the players are looking tired and jaded. That affects their commitment. They have gone into a game which is not as demanding at League and they have had too easy a time.

I am not knocking Rugby Union because it is a game in its own right but League is much faster and more physical. I played with good players who came out of Rugby Union. They all agreed that League is much more physically demanding and you have to be mentally sharper. They would say they could play three games of Union compared with one game of League.

I think it is time for a whole new approach to the game in Britain. We have got to start leading again rather than just following the Australians. They are too far advanced and we will never catch up to them. We need to look at other methods and say to hell with the Australians, we are going to do our own thing.

We are not dedicated enough in Britain, and we have a tendency to be lazy, while the Australians go out and get things done. It took us years in this country to introduce Rugby League to schools, where as Down Under by the age of 12 kids have had a fantastic grooming and all they have to be coached in is the game plan and the will to win. That is what we are up against. We have to find new ways of developing our game in Britain.

We need a man with bottle to take the lead. I would love the opportunity. I would jump at the chance to coach Great Britain.

THE CHARLTON ALL-STARS

I have had the pleasure and privilege not only of watching but also playing against some of the greatest Rugby League players in the world. To pick my all-time favourite 13 was tougher than any team selection I ever had to make as a coach. I pondered over it for hours before I came up with the definitive side. And let me tell you, this is some team!

It evoked memories of great players of yesteryear. Legends I grew up watching and dreaming I would be like as a player. Dick Huddart was my childhood hero and he takes me back to a golden era for Rugby League.

The awesome talent of these players would surely earn them a place, not just in my all-star team, but also in the Rugby League hall of fame. They have a combination of individual talent and all-round ability which separates them from the rest. It would be frightening to think what a team like this could achieve had they all been put together.

GRAHAM LANGLANDS
Fullback. St George and Australia.

Australian Test rugby's most prolific points scorer who burst on to the scene in 1962. Scored a record 104 points in Anglo/Australian Tests and his total of 43 goals is the highest number recorded by any Australian player against Great Britain.

This guy had so much ability and skill, he came immediately to mind and would have to be my first choice for position one.

His strengths were his ability to tackle and run the ball and also his ability to beat opponents. His goal kicking skill spoke for itself and he also had the knack of being in the right place at the right time.

I played against "Changa" regularly in Test matches and for my clubs against touring sides. I remember playing in a Test match in 1974 at Lang Park, Brisbane. Australia beat us 12-6. We then played another in Sydney and we won and had to go into a decider in the third Test.

We were winning by one point with just three minutes to go. Ron Coote made a break and gave the ball to Langlands. He made a full-length dive at the corner flag which clinched it for Australia. The game had been won but that wasn't enough for Changa. He still had to go and kick the conversion. It was like him saying: "Take that you pommy!"

He put the ball down and kicked it from the touchline. There was no way back for us from that.

He was a complete professional and a great ambassador for his country. I know him personally and he's a smashing bloke. He also likes a beer!

I also considered two other Australians, Graham Eadie and Les Johns, for the full-back position. They were also quality players.

BILLY BOSTON
Right Winger. Wigan, Blackpool Borough and Great Britain.

A block-busting winger of the Fifties and Sixties, who scored 571 tries in a distinguished career. Winning the first of his 31 Great Britain caps in the second Test against Australia in the 1954 tour, he went on to break the tour try-scoring record with 36 tries and equal the record scored in a Test match with four against New Zealand in Auckland.

Billy was the only player I considered for this position. He was a huge, powerful player, who was also very quick for a big man. He was an awesome opponent. He was as wide as a house – a very difficult man to pull down.

He played for Great Britain before my time but I played against him when I was a youngster coming through the ranks and he was a veteran.

Yet off the field he was such a gentleman. A very special man.

REG GASNIER
Right Centre. St George and Australia.

Won 36 caps for Australia and made a huge impact on the British scene in 1959 when his performances earned him the reputation as one of the world's finest centres.

He had all the qualities a Rugby League player needs and not one aspect of his game was weak. He was ideally built for the position of centre and had so much pace and skill. He was also a good defensive player. Reg was a formidable opponent, who would get you in a certain position and then change direction before you could blink.

He was a very nice fella off the field and on it he was so competitive, he would even want to win at tiddlywinks!

Reg was a very similar player to another Australian, Andrew Ettinghausen, who I also regard very highly.

NEIL FOX
Left Centre. Wakefield Trinity, Bradford Northern, Hull KR, York, Bramley, Huddersfield and Great Britain.

Made 828 appearances for club, county and at international level, amassing 6,220 points, consisting of 358 tries and 2,575 goals.

He was a very powerful player, who wasn't quite as skilful as Gasnier but could break the line with his sheer power. It was his power, which came from his upper body, rather than his skill which stands out for me. Fox was the model professional in my eyes.

The only other player who came to mind for this position was Paul Newlove, of St Helens, who is a similar type of player. But where Newlove doesn't kick goals, Neil Fox was an exceptional kicker.

TOM VAN VOLLENHOVEN
Left Wing. St Helens.
Former South African rugby union player who proved a sensation for South Africa in the Test series against the British Lions in 1955. Switched codes to join St Helens in 1957.

This legendary player had great pace. He could run from one end of the pitch to the other and wouldn't tire. He would be just as fast at the end of his run as he was when he took off. He could beat anyone when he was in full flight.

In my all-star team there would be a beautiful blend of the power of Neil Fox and the finishing of Tom Van Vollenhoven. I played for Workington against him and he really was something special. St Helens rated him very highly.

For this position, obviously I had to think very carefully about including Martin Offiah, of whom I am a great admirer. He sells the game very well, is a great ambassador and I don't think there are enough personalities like him.

Early in his career, I felt Martin's defence was sub-standard, although he has got his act together now but Tom Van Vollenhoven had those defensive qualities right from the start and that swayed me towards him.

BOBBY FULTON
Stand-off. Manly, Eastern Suburbs, Warrington and Australia.

English-born but raised in Australia and was part of the Kangaroos' Tours of Europe in 1973 and 1978, the latter as captain. Formerly Australia's national coach.

I played against "Bozo" on quite a few occasions and he was the king-pin of the side, around whom everything revolved. He was a very strong and skilful player with razor-sharp acceleration, who could adjust to any situation which was the sign of a class player.

I remember playing for Cumbria against Australia at Barrow in the late Seventies and I went in the toilets. He was sitting on the toilet with the door open and he called out: "Hey Charlo, how you going on mate?" I can remember standing beside him while he was in the loo for about five or ten minutes talking about our respective teams. To anyone who came in, it must have looked so funny. It was so typical of "Bozo" because he was such a character off the field. Anyway we went on to lose quite convincingly that day.

The only other player I considered for this position was Alan Hardisty, of Castleford. "Chuck" was more skilful than Bobby Fulton, but Bobby got the nod because he combined power and skill.

ALEX MURPHY

Scrum-half. St Helens, Leigh, Warrington and Great Britain.

Gained 26 international caps in a distinguished career. Had coaching spells at Leigh, Warrington, Wigan and St Helens, taking them all to Challenge Cup finals and won every trophy and honour available.

"Spud" oozed class. He was a brilliant player who had everything. He had so much pace and ability and his tackling was out of this world. If you looked at him now you would wonder to yourself how he played Rugby League but he certainly did and he was one of the best at it.

If today's players want to model themselves on someone they wouldn't go far wrong if they followed Alex.

We had tremendous respect for each other as players and get on extremely well. We would go on the field and knock hell out of each other and that's where respect comes from in Rugby League. It is a bond and friendship comes from that. Alex's name was the first I put down on this team because I don't think there is any player to rival him.

ARTIE BEETSON

Prop. Redcliffe, Balmain, Hull KR, Eastern Suburbs and Australia.

Giant 6ft 2in, 16st Aussie who won 10 caps in Anglo-Australian Test matches. Had one season in England with Hull KR, before returning Down Under in 1971.

I have come across a few notable open side props in my time but the one who stands out in my mind is Artie Beetson. He was one of the first Australian prop forwards to have ball skills. He could also take players on, off-load the ball well and was a terrific tackler.

For a big man his skills were unbelievable. He also had all the qualities of a good leader, which is why the Australians selected him as captain. During his time at Hull KR, his skills seemed to be so advanced compared with other Australian players of his generation.

GEORGE PEPONIS
Hooker. Canterbury and Australia.

Another Australian captain with all the attributes needed to lead a side. As a player, George was a strong-running hooker and good runner from dummy half, who was also an outstanding tackler and footballer. Over the passage of time, not many players come along who have half his ability, and I can't think of many hookers who were as strong, skilful and pacey.

He was also a hard man, physically tough in an uncompromising game. I remember you could knock him down and he would just pick himself up as if nothing had happened.

CLIFF WATSON
Prop forward. St Helens, Cronulla, Wollongong and Great Britain.

Cockney-born prop who began his career as a Rugby Union player in the Midlands, before responding to a newspaper advert for players to join St Helens. A key player of the 1966 tour of Australia and the 1968 World Cup party which travelled to Australia and New Zealand.

A big, strong man, who was rarely out of the spotlight following his conversion to the 13-man game. The Aussies absolutely feared him because he was so tough and wouldn't take a backward step.

The word awesome springs to mind and if you ever saw his face, you would know exactly why. He had been smashed around the face so many times by opponent's elbows, he looked like a heavyweight boxer. Yet off the field, behind those looks was a real gentleman.

DICK HUDDART
Second row. Whitehaven, St Helens, St George and Great Britain.

A member of the all-conquering Great Britain tour of Australia in 1958 where he collected 17 tries. Also a member of the 1962 tour before his transfer Down Under robbed England of one of its finest players.

Dick was a Flimby boy Cumbria could be proud of. He had a tremendous turn of pace and was also a good tackler. He could catch backs other players were incapable of touching.

It was that pace which meant he was another player the Australians feared. I regarded him as brilliant. I am also lucky enough to regard Dick and his family, who now live on the Gold Coast, as friends.

BRIAN EDGAR
Second row. Workington Town and Great Britain.

Represented England Schools at Rugby Union before switching codes. A veteran of three Great Britain tours, captaining them in 1966 in all three Tests against Australia.

Brian was a gentle giant blessed with all the attributes of a great player. He was a big, powerful man but he still had a fine turn of speed. He was also a master at distributing the ball. He could step off either foot, go through a gap and release the ball.

I used to watch Brian and players like him and dream I could be as good as them. He was one of my idols and I used to really look up to him when I first started playing. Brian was captain of Workington when I first joined them. He was a mentor to me and would help and guide me into good habits. I learned a lot from playing alongside a great man like him.

WAYNE PEARCE
Loose forward. Balmain and Australia.

A one club player who made a huge impact in Australia's 1982 tour of Europe. A human battering ram with a reputation as a fitness fanatic. If young players today chose to model themselves on Wayne Pearce, they wouldn't go far wrong.

We heard stories how, after strenuous training sessions under coach Frank Stanton, Wayne ran up and down a full flight of stairs at their hotel in Leeds. He was apparently hyperactive and just couldn't sit still.

As a player he was sheer class. He wasn't a big guy and was very quick, but still possessed a lot of defensive qualities. He picked up a nasty injury which forced him to miss out on a tour. He retired quite young and was a big loss to the game.

TRIBUTES

ALEX MURPHY
Former St Helens, Leigh, Warrington and Great Britain scrum-half.

Paul was a great player at the highest level. He had pace and that unpre-dictability which made him a very difficult opponent, but he was also a great defender.

He absolutely loved the game and had tremendous enthusiasm which is so important. Off the field he was a great bloke and we got on very well and really admired each other. I have a lot of respect for the man.

He was a superstar ordinary people could talk to, which is very unusual today.

REGGIE PARKER
Former Barrow and England second row forward and 1974 British Lions Tour manager

Ken Traill once said: "There are good players, great players and Willie Horne". I would say the same about Paul Charlton.

Players come and go and are easily forgotten but Paul will go down in history as one of the all-time greats.

He played during a golden era for Rugby League and was absolutely tremendous on that 1974 Tour. I can still picture him now taking a bomb.

After just about every game on that Tour he came off injured because he had given 100 per cent but you knew damn well he would be able to play in the next game. He would have treatment and be ready to do battle for Britain again. He was a very committed player who shirked nothing.

I used to go and watch him play for Salford, and it was amazing to see him and that wonderful back line full of internationals. They were so exciting to watch. Friday nights up at Salford were really something special.

He should have played international rugby much sooner than he did because he was more than good enough but he was out on a limb up in Workington and didn't hit the big time until he went to Salford.

DAVID WATKINS
Ex-Wales RU, Salford, Swinton and Great Britain

I first recognised Paul's qualities as a Rugby League player when he was still playing for Workington and I played against him for Salford. There were no doubts in my mind, or my club's, that he was going to be a great player and Salford were very keen to sign him.

Suddenly here was a player who was equal to anything in the world but, because Rugby League didn't have a high profile, I don't think people outside the game appreciated just how good he was.

He had outrageous talents. He was a prolific scorer and he showed the speed, anticipation and awareness to score 33 tries in a season, still a world record for a full-back.

A lot of people say that if he was such a prolific try scorer, there must have been some defensive deficiencies. But there weren't. In a one-on-one, he would inevitably nail them.

On the field he was full of himself in a confident rather than a boastful way and always very much his own man.

RAY FRENCH
Former Great Britain, St Helens and Widnes

Paul was one of Rugby League's most dependable players, who relished playing every week and took a huge pride in his performance.

He was a very strong player, not only a brilliant attacker but also equally talented defensively.

He gave 100 per cent and his zest and enthusiasm were fantastic. It continued into his coaching career, although sadly the hard work he put in at Carlisle has not come to fruition because of the merger with Barrow.

RON MORGAN
Former Whitehaven coach and Cumberland team manager and secretary

As a player I would rate him as the best full-back I have ever seen and as a person he is one of the nicest fellas I've ever met.

I have never heard anyone say a bad word about Paul Charlton. There are not many people in life about whom you can say that.

He was a great leader and the players had huge respect for him. I can still picture him now in the Cumberland dressing room banging the ball on the table and shouting: "Come on lads, we can beat these lot".

He was a player I would dearly have loved to sign when I was

Whitehaven coach. I knew he was unsettled at Workington and I would have loved to have tempted him to the Recreation Ground, but there was no way we could compete with Salford.

He was one of the most loyal players I ever met when he played under me for Cumberland. Cumberland always had the first County Championship match of the season because we had no floodlights and the match would always coincide with the lead up to the semi-final of the County Cups. My phone would be red-hot with players from the glamour clubs crying off because their teams had paid them not to play but Paul never pulled out.

His strengths were his counter-attack and his sharpness. As soon as he got the ball you would see him weighing up his options, whereas the other full-backs would be lumbering forward.

We went to a lot of club dinners together and he was always very approachable. There was no edge to him even though he was a star in his hey-day with Salford.

After his playing career was over, he wasn't too proud to come back and be a junior coach and then 'A' team coach at Carlisle. How many ex-Great Britain players would do that?

IKE SOUTHWARD
Former Workington Town, Oldham, Cumberland and Great Britain winger.

I have never in my entire Rugby League career met anyone as dedicated to the game as Paul. He was to Rugby League what Geoff Boycott was to cricket. He was totally disciplined and dedicated right from the day he joined Town.

Having Paul in the team was like having a third centre. He could score tries from anywhere. He knew where he was going even before he had the ball and could spot a gap so easily.

Next to me in the dressing room, Paul used to be up and down and I would have to tell him to sit still. I think he was psyching himself up rather than suffering nerves.

We also played cricket against each other, and he was a good bowler. When he used to bowl to me I used to stick my tongue out and Paul would collapse into giggles and wouldn't be able to bowl.

ARNOLD "BOXER" WALKER
Former Workington Town, Whitehaven, Cumberland, England and Great Britain scrum-half.

When people ask me who I respect in Rugby League, the first name that comes to mind is Paul Charlton. If he was playing today, he would still be the number one full-back.

Despite his star status, he never forgot his roots and, when he returned to Workington from Salford, I found out just how big a friend he was to me. We had some huge arguments about Rugby League, but we were great friends at the end of the day.

We were part of a cracking side which won the Lancashire Cup in 1977, and if that team had stayed together we could have gone on to win at Wembley.

Paul is a Kells lad, the same as me, and he groomed me as a player and really stood by me.

He was the most dedicated player I have ever known. While I would be out having a few pints, he would be in bed by 8pm but he knew what I was like. He always used to tell me there was plenty of time for wine, women and song after my career was over. I wish I had taken notice of him!

PETER GORLEY
Former Workington Town, St Helens, Cumberland, England and Great Britain prop.

We used to hear stories about how when we had lost a match Paul would go and do extra training on St Bees beach. He took losing very badly, and would really take it to heart. That was what made him a great player.

I could count only on one hand the number of bad games he had. Everybody liked Paul because he was easy to get on with, and I've never known anybody fall out with him.

As a coach he was well respected because of what he had achieved in the game and because of his fitness and dedication.

One match against Wakefield Trinity stands out in my mind. They were a fair team but we were winning with just a couple minutes to go. If they had scored they still could have beaten us. Dave Topliss, who was a very good player, very classy and fast, broke through the Workington line with only Paul to beat.

If he had beaten Paul he would have scored but Paul just put him exactly where he wanted him. He shepherded him to the touchline and caught him right on the corner flag. That incident just summed him up; he was a class player who did class things. That incident was worth the admission fee alone.

ROBERT GATE
Rugby League historian

Paul Charlton is arguably the finest full-back to have been produced in Cumbria and that is saying a lot when his predecessors included Bill Eagers, Bobbie Scott, Jim Brough, Billy Holding, John McKeown and Syd Lowden. Certainly as an attacking, try-scoring full-back, the region has never seen his equal and if he were playing in the modern game he would be in his element, without doubt in the superstar bracket.

In the purple period of his career, Paul was recognised as the world's top full-back. His attacking play was simply stunning and the game has never see a full-back who scored tries in such a torrent. He was more than an attacking machine, however. He was a magnificent defender too. His speed enabled him to cut down even the quickest wingers and he had that unteachable knack of being able to shepherd ball-carriers where he wanted them.

Paul was one of the giants of Rugby League. Only six men in the entire history of the sport have played more first-class games than Paul's 727 in a career which lasted 20 years and certainly no full-back has come anywhere near matching his tally of 223 tries. Unless the game changes, no full-back ever will.

ALF WILLIAMS
Lifelong friend and secretary of Kells ARL Vice Presidents' Club.

If I had a son who wanted to be a Rugby League player, I couldn't pick a better role model for him than Paul Charlton.

Paul was one of the best full-backs ever. He was also one of the most dedicated people I have ever known. Any aspiring young player should try to model themselves on Paul.

I have known him all his life since we were children growing up together in Whitehaven and he hasn't altered from that day to this.

He is a smashing bloke and it is a privilege and an honour to call him my friend.

JIM KITCHEN
Former secretary and chairman of Kells ARL.

The reason Paul was such a great player was because he was so dedicated. He was also a fitness fanatic who didn't drink or smoke and just lived for the game. I could see straight-away Paul had potential. He had something the other players didn't have – plenty of pace.

When he first joined Kells you could see immediately he was going to make the grade with a big club, and that was why I recommended him to Workington Town.

HENRY BROWN
Former Kells, Cumberland and Great Britain amateur fullback.

Even at an early age Paul showed a lot of potential. He was a skinny kid and I always felt he could have done with being a bit bigger but it never prevented him from reaching the top.

He was very fast off the mark and a very elusive player who was a tough opponent. I wanted to get him involved with Kells' young side because I felt if we didn't, he was going to be a real handful as an opponent if he went to another team like Hensingham or Egremont.

Whether he was playing for Kells, Workington Town, Salford or Great Britain, Paul would go on the field and give 100 per cent. I rate him as one of the great full-backs, who had real attacking flair. He was also a master at selling a dummy.

JACK McNAMARA
Manchester Evening News *Rugby League writer 1956-92.*

Paul Charlton was one of the finest post-war full-backs. He was a devastating tackler but even more impressive was his attacking work. He could come into the line with such force and power, and created plenty of tries for others as well as himself. He was a wonderful fielder of the ball and his positional play was near perfect.

We knew Salford had signed a winner. He was already an outstanding player with Workington and everyone was thrilled when he signed for Salford and settled in very quickly.

Off the field, he was a delightful person, a man everybody respected as a first-class sportsman and a gentleman. He was also very modest and will probably blush at these tributes, but he deserves every kind word said about him.

He's a first-class chap and he remains to this day a very popular and admired figure. The older Salford fans always say there was no one like Paul Charlton and they still think the world of him.

TOM MITCHELL
The late president of Workington Town.

Paul had a brilliant career. His 33 tries in a season from the full-back position was a world record and is never likely to be broken.

He was some player. There were not many like him. I was very upset with his departure from the club but in the end it was outside any influence I could have used.

RAY EDGAR
Former Commercial Manager of Carlisle Border Raiders.

I would love to see Paul given a coaching job at a top Super League club and be in the game full-time. He would be so good for the game, and I think he would be one of the country's top coaches.

I don't think I've ever met anyone quite like Paul. I've never known anybody so enthusiastic about Rugby League in my life. I think at Carlisle he would have had the players training on Christmas Day if he could have done!

He was a 100 per cent winner and they say he was the same as a player, although I was never lucky enough to see him play.

He would take defeat badly and blame himself, but he always went into the bar to have a bottle of beer and chat to supporters, win or lose.

GEORGE GRAHAM
Former Carlisle Border Raiders prop and Newcastle Falcons and Scotland prop.

Paul is a legend in Rugby League and he was hugely respected by his players. He was a hard fitness coach. He was as fit as us and would do the training we did even though he was well into his fifties.

PAUL CHARLTON'S PLAYING CAREER

TEST APPEARANCES

Oct 23 1965	GB 15 New Zealand 9 at Odsal	
Oct 31 1970	GB 27 New Zealand 17 at Swinton *	World Cup
Feb 6 1972	GB 10 France 9 at Toulouse	
Mar 12 1972	GB 45 France 10 at Odsal	TRY
Oct 29 1972	GB 27 Australia 21 at Perpignan	World Cup
Nov 1 1972	GB 13 France 4 at Grenoble	World Cup
Nov 4 1972	GB 53 New Zealand 19 at Pau TRY	World Cup
Nov 11 1972	GB 10 Australia 10 at Lyons	World Cup F'1
Nov 3 1973	GB 21 Australia 12 at Wembley	
Nov 24 1973	GB 6 Australia 14 at Leeds	
Dec 1 1973	GB 5 Australia 15 at Warrington	
Jan 20 1974	GB 24 France 5 at Grenoble	
Feb 17 1974	GB 29 France 0 at Wigan	2 TRIES
Jun 15 1974	GB 6 Australia 12 at Brisbane	
Jul 6 1974	GB 16 Australia 11 at Sydney	
Jul 20 1974	GB 18 Australia 22 at Sydney	
Jul 27 1974	GB 8 New Zealand 13 at Auckland	
Aug 4 1974	GB 17 New Zealand 8 at Christchurch	
Aug 10 1974	GB 20 New Zealand 0 at Auckland	

* Substitute

ENGLAND APPEARANCE

Mar 16 1975	England 20 France 2 at Leeds	World Championship

GREAT BRITAIN ON 1974 TOUR (excluding Tests)

May 26	GB 41 Darwin 2	TRY
Jun 4	GB 24 Wide-Bay 12	TRY
Jun 9	GB 13 Queensland 12	
Jun 18	GB 15 Brisbane 20	
Jun 23	GB 38 Northern NSW 14	2 TRIES
Jun 26	GB 25 Western NSW 10	
Jun 29	GB 9 NSW13	
Jun 30	GB 26 Illawarra 22	
Jul 7	GB 34 Monaro 7	
Jul 10	GB 36 Riverina 10*	
Jul 30	GB 19 Maoris 16	

* Substitute

1974 GREAT BRITAIN TOUR OF AUSTRALIA AND NEW ZEALAND

Tour party
Manager: Reggie Parker (Blackpool Borough)
Coach: Jim Challinor (St Helens)
Captain: Chris Hesketh (Salford)

	Apps	Tries	Goals	Points
K Ashcroft (Warrington)	14	2	0	6
J Atkinson (Leeds)	8	8	0	24
A Bates (Dewsbury)	17	2	0	6
J Bates (Dewsbury)	6	0	0	0
J Bevan (Warrington)	17	15	0	45
K Bridges (Featherstone R)	8	0	0	0
J Butler (Rochdale)	18	6	0	18
P CHARLTON (SALFORD)	17	4	0	12
E Chisnall (St Helens)	18	3	0	9
T Clawson (Oldham)	13	0	24	48
C Dixon (Salford)	19	4	0	12
L Dyl (Leeds)	17	14	0	42
D Eckersley (St Helens)	13	3	12	33
K Gill (Salford)	16	8	0	24
J Gray (Wigan)	17	2	53(1)	111
C Hesketh (Salford)	20	4	0	12
J Mills (Widnes)	16	2	0	6
R Millward (Hull KR)	12	8	18	60
S Nash (Featherstone R)	16	5	1(1)	16
G Nicholls (St Helens)	18	4	0	12
S Norton (Castleford)	17	5	0	15
*W Ramsey (Bradford N)	7	2	5	16
D Redfearn (Bradford N)	18	18	2	58
*M Richards (Salford)	10	5	0	15
P Rose (Hull KR)	14	5	0	15
J Thompson (Featherstone R)	21	1	0	3
D Watkins (Salford)	8	2	12	30
D Willicombe (Wigan)	15	8	0	24

J Challinor made one appearance and scored a try.
Appearances include substitute appearances.

* Replacement for players injured on tour.

CUMBERLAND COUNTY APPEARANCES

Sep 8 1965	Cumb 19 Yorkshire 3	at Hull KR
Sep 20 1965	Cumb 14 Lancashire 11	at Whitehaven
Sep 7 1966	Cumb 17 Yorkshire 17	at Workington
Oct 12 1966	Cumb 18 Lancashire 14	at Warrington 3 goals
Sep 12 1967	Cumb 6 Lancashire 19	at Workington
Oct 25 1967	Cumb 23 Yorkshire 34	at Castleford 4 goals
Nov 18 1967	Cumb 17 Australians 15	at Workington
Sep 11 1968	Cumb 10 Yorkshire 23	at Whitehaven
Nov 6 1968	Cumb 19 Lancashire 24	at St Helens
Sep 24 1969	Cumb 10 Lancashire 30	at Workington +
Oct 1 1969	Cumb 3 Yorkshire 42	at Hull KR
Sep 14 1970	Cumb 21 Yorkshire 15	at Whitehaven
Nov 11 1970	Cumb 5 Lancashire 28	at Barrow+
Sep 15 1971	Cumb 17 Lancashire 7	at Workington+ 3 goals
Oct 20 1971	Cumb12 Yorkshire 17	at Wakefield+
Sep 13 1972	Cumb 23 Yorkshire 14	at Whitehaven+
Sep 27 1972	Cumb 16 Lancashire 26	at Warrington+ Try
Jan 17 1973	Cumb 7 Yorkshire 20	at Leeds+ play-off
Sep 5 1973	Cumb 6 Lancashire 18	at Barrow+
Sep 12 1973	Cumb 12 Yorkshire 37	at Bramley+
Oct 24 1973	Cumb 2 Australians 28	at Whitehaven+
Sep 11 1974	Cumb 10 Yorkshire 7	at Workington+ 2 tries
Sep 18 1974	Cumb 4 Lancashire 29	at Warrington+
Sep 25 1974	Cumb 19 Other Nat's 12	at Whitehaven+
Nov 19 1975	Cumb 7 Yorkshire 10	at Dewsbury+
Feb 2 1977	Cumb 14 Lancashire 18	at Leigh+
Feb 15 1977	Cumb 12 Yorkshire 12	at Whitehaven+ Try
Oct 5 1977	Cumb 10 Yorkshire 28	at York+
Sep 20 1978	Cumb 9 Yorkshire 37	at Hull+
Oct 1 1978	Cumb 4 Australians 47	at Barrow+
Oct 11 1978	Cumb 16 Lancashire 15	at Whitehaven+
Sep 5 1979	Cumb 15 Lancashire 23	at St Helens*

+ Captain

* Substitute

All Paul Charlton's games for Cumberland/Cumbria were as full-back except for the game against Yorkshire at Dewsbury in 1975 when he appeared at centre.

The county team was titled Cumberland until the 1973-74 season after which it became known as Cumbria.

RECORD IN CLUB RUGBY LEAGUE 1961-1981

WORKINGTON TOWN Debut: 23 Sept, 1961 v Rochdale Hornets (A)

	A	T	G	P
1961-62	1	–	–	–
1962-63	10	1	–	3
1963-64	28	3	–	9
1964-65	40	11	–	33
1965-66	36	14	28	98
1966-67	32+2	10	3	36
1967-68	39+1	13	6	51
1968-69	40	18	37	128
1969-70	15	9	3	33
TOTALS	241+3	79	77	391

SALFORD Debut: 29 Oct, 1969 v St Helens (H)

	A	T	G	P
1969-70	26	4	1	14
1970-71	38	17	–	51
1971-72	42	18	–	54
1972-73	44	31	1	95
1973-74	44	15	–	45
1974-75	39+1	14	–	42
TOTALS	233+1	99	2	301

WORKINGTON TOWN Debut: 17 Aug, 1975 v Hull (A)

	A	T	G	P
1975-76	26+1	8	–	24
1976-77	41	8	–	24
1977-78	36	6	–	18
1978-79	32	2	–	6
1979-80	36	7	–	21
1980-81	3	–	–	–
TOTALS	174+1	31	–	93

BLACKPOOL BOROUGH Debut: 1 Feb, 1981 v Whitehaven (H)

	A	T	G	P
1980-81	10+1	2	–	6

Final game: Blackpool Borough 8 Wigan 23, on 20 Apr, 1981 – try

CAREER RECORD

	A	T	G	P
Workington Town	415+4	110	77	484
Salford	233+1	99	2	301
Blackpool Borough	10+1	2	-	6
Tests	18+1	4	-	12
England	1		-	-
1974 GB Tour	10+1	4	-	12
Cumberland	31+1	4	10	32
TOTAL	718+9	223	89	847

DOMESTIC HONOURS

1973-74	Championship winner – Salford	
21 Oct 1972	Lancashire Cup	Salford 25 Swinton 11 Try
13 Oct 1973	Lancashire Cup	Salford 9 Wigan 19
2 Nov 1974	Lancashire Cup	Salford 2 Widnes 6
30 Oct 1976	Lancashire Cup+	Workington Town 11 Widnes 16
29 Oct 1977	Lancashire Cup+	Workington Town 16 Wigan 13
7 Oct 1978	Lancashire Cup+	Workington Town 13 Widnes 15
8 Dec 1979	Lancashire Cup+	Workington Town 0 Widnes 11

| 24 Mar 1973 | Players Trophy | Salford 7 Leeds 12 |

| 17 Dec 1974 | Floodlit Trophy | Salford 7 Leeds 12 |

(Paul missed the replay which Salford won 10-5 on 28 Jan, 1975)

| 1975-76 | Promotion – Workington Town |

+ Captain

ACKNOWLEDGEMENTS

Thank you to Paul for entrusting me with telling the story of his career and for giving me the opportunity to fulfil a lifetime's ambition in writing a book.

I hope I have honoured the trust you placed in me and done justice to your career and standing in the game of Rugby League.

Thank you to Lillian for allowing me to "borrow" Paul every Saturday morning for two months while we looked back on his career, and to Gary and Harold Charlton for their insight into his family life.

Thanks to Alf Williams for sharing the memories of growing up with Paul in Woodhouse, and for help in organising photographs.

Also to Jim Kitchen, Henry Brown and Tom Mitchell, three men who played such a big part in spotting Paul's early potential, for providing me with photographs and invaluable information about his early career.

Thank you to Arnold "Boxer" Walker. That evening we spent chatting in the bar at Kells amateur rugby league club was an unforgettable experience!

Also thanks to Peter Gorley for his stories about his days playing with Paul at Workington Town and his memories of the team's heroics in the 1977 Lancashire Cup final win. Thanks also to another ex-Town player Phil Kitchin.

Thanks to former Great Britain team manager Reggie Parker for his entertaining tales of Paul's glorious international career and the loan of photographs.

To Ray Edgar and Alan Tucker for the information on Paul's time with Carlisle Border Raiders.

Thank you to former Cumberland coach Ron Morgan for his kindness in taking the time and trouble to share his memories with me even during his illness.

Thank you to Ike and Betty Southward for their warm hospitality, memories, loan of books, cups of tea and for helping me caption photographs.

Thank you to Robert Gate, Rugby League's official historian, for providing me with all the statistics on Paul's career, match reports and for casting an expert eye over the manuscript.

Thanks to Paul's ex-Salford, Workington and Cumberland team-mate Tony Colloby for the loan of his match programmes.

To Workington Town's historian Joe Holliday and Salford's

statistician Darryl Platt for background information.

Thank you to the hugely-talented artist Stuart Smith for the fantastic paintings to illustrate the cover and to Sky TV's Mike Stephenson for taking the time to provide an entertaining foreword.

Thank you to my employers Cumbrian Newspapers for the use of photographs and to my editor Keith Sutton for granting me permission to borrow them.

Thanks to Jonnie Becker at the Cumbrian Gazette for the use of the Tom Mitchell photograph. The older photographs were anonymous and so my sincere apologies for not being able to give worthy credit to the photographers who took them.

Thanks to Elizabeth Kay, Cumbrian Newspapers' appeals co-ordinator, and promotions manager David McNeill for their help in arranging advertising and sales of the book through the Heartbeat 100 Appeal.

Thank you to colleague Paul Creber for his time and care in editing the manuscript and to deputy sports editor Mike Gardner for advice and for proof reading the book.

A special thanks to friends Dave Gudgeon, Joanne Burgess and Tony Wilson for their support and for taking the time to proof read the book.

Finally thank you to Joyce and Bill Little without whose love and support this story would never have been told. No daughter could ever ask for better parents.